CONTROVERSIES

Women in Politics

WITHDRAWN

Other Books in the Current Controversies Series

Women in Politics

Debra A. Miller, Book Editor

GREENHAVEN PRESS

A part of Gale, Cengage Learning

Detroit • New York • San Francisco • New Haven, Conn • Waterville, Maine • London

Elizabeth Des Chenes, *Director, Publishing Solutions*

© 2013 Greenhaven Press, a part of Gale, Cengage Learning

Gale and Greenhaven Press are registered trademarks used herein under license.

For more information, contact:
Greenhaven Press
27500 Drake Rd.
Farmington Hills, MI 48331-3535
Or you can visit our Internet site at gale.cengage.com

Articles in Greenhaven Press anthologies are often edited for length to meet page requirements. In addition, original titles of these works are changed to clearly present the main thesis and to explicitly indicate the author's opinion. Every effort is made to ensure that Greenhaven Press accurately reflects the original intent of the authors. Every effort has been made to trace the owners of copyrighted material.

Cover image © eurobanks/Shutterstock.com.

LIBRARY OF CONGRESS CATALOGING-IN-PUBLICATION DATA

Women in politics / Debra A. Miller, book editor.
    p. cm. -- (Current controversies)
    Includes bibliographical references and index.
    ISBN 978-0-7377-6249-5 (hardcover) -- ISBN 978-0-7377-6250-1 (pbk.)
    1. Women--Political activity--United States--Juvenile literature. 2. Women politicians--United States--Juvenile literature. 3. Women political candidates--United States--Juvenile literature. 4. Women and democracy--United States--Juvenile literature. 5. Women--Political activity--Juvenile literature. 6. Women and democracy--Juvenile literature. I. Miller, Debra A.
    HQ1236.5.U6W6628 2012
    320.73082--dc23
                                                            2012009509

Printed in the United States of America
  2 3 4 5 6   16 15 14 13 12

FD300

Contents

Chapter 1: Have Women Made Substantial Gains in US Politics?

Yes: Women Have Made Substantial Gains in US Politics

In 2008, a woman—Hillary Clinton—was almost elected president, and there were modest gains for women in the US Congress, with women gaining one seat in the Senate and three in the House. And in the states, a record number of women ran for office in a presidential election year, resulting in an increase in the number of women serving in state legislatures, from 23.7 percent to 24.2 percent. Women's advocates hope these examples will encourage a new generation of women to run for office.

No: Women Have Not Made Substantial Gains in US Politics

Although more women ran for US Congress than ever before in the 2010 midterm elections, the election resulted in a decline in the number of women in Congress from 17 percent to 16 percent—the first decrease in thirty years. In addition, many female members of Congress lost leadership roles as Republicans took over the House of Representatives—most notably Representative Nancy Pelosi (D-CA), who was the first woman to become Speaker of the House. Women, however, made progress in state gubernatorial races, where three states elected their first female governors.

Martha Coakley's failure to win a Senate seat in the 2010 Massachusetts special election is one of the latest reminders of how far women have to go to be equal with men in US politics. About 216 women ran for the House and the Senate in 2010, far below 251—the number of women who ran for Congress in 1992. The main problem is that not enough women are running for office, partly due to sexist media coverage of candidates.

Chapter 2: What Is the Status of Women in World Politics?

Women are winning some of the most powerful political positions in some the largest nations in the world. Examples include German Chancellor Angela Merkel, US Secretary of State Hillary Clinton, and Brazilian President Dilma Rousseff. Although women still have a long way to go, these examples show that women can be competent leaders and that people are ready to elect them or appoint them to positions of great power.

Women have made progress around the world in various fields, including politics. Women now hold top political jobs in a number of countries, but even in the developed world, women remain far below men in political power. It is difficult to measure the impact of women in politics, because there have been so few female politicians. But it is clear that liberating women helps boost the economies of countries and the world.

Chapter 3: Does the Participation of Women Improve Politics?

Yes: The Participation of Women Does Improve Politics

No: The Participation of Women Does Not Improve Politics

Many women think that more women in politics will mean more attention will be paid to women's issues such as child care and equal pay. The 2010 midterm elections dispelled this notion as many conservative women were elected into legislatures. Women candidates such as former Alaska Governor Sarah Palin, Representative Michele Bachmann (R-MN), and others are more concerned with government debt and excessive regulation, so it is no longer safe to assume that electing women will further the cause of women's issues.

Chapter 4: What Steps Should Be Taken to Encourage More Women to Enter Politics?

The future of politics lies with women who are now graduating from college. In order for women to achieve equal representation in government, the barriers must be surmounted with active, early recruitment and training of girls and young women. A number of programs are already working to achieve these goals, and today's graduates should consider politics as a potential career.

Foreword

By definition, controversies are "discussions of questions in which opposing opinions clash" (*Webster's Twentieth Century Dictionary Unabridged*). Few would deny that controversies are a pervasive part of the human condition and exist on virtually every level of human enterprise. Controversies transpire between individuals and among groups, within nations and between nations. Controversies supply the grist necessary for progress by providing challenges and challengers to the status quo. They also create atmospheres where strife and warfare can flourish. A world without controversies would be a peaceful world; but it also would be, by and large, static and prosaic.

The Series' Purpose

The purpose of the Current Controversies series is to explore many of the social, political, and economic controversies dominating the national and international scenes today. Titles selected for inclusion in the series are highly focused and specific. For example, from the larger category of criminal justice, Current Controversies deals with specific topics such as police brutality, gun control, white collar crime, and others. The debates in Current Controversies also are presented in a useful, timeless fashion. Articles and book excerpts included in each title are selected if they contribute valuable, long-range ideas to the overall debate. And wherever possible, current information is enhanced with historical documents and other relevant materials. Thus, while individual titles are current in focus, every effort is made to ensure that they will not become quickly outdated. Books in the Current Controversies series will remain important resources for librarians, teachers, and students for many years.

In addition to keeping the titles focused and specific, great care is taken in the editorial format of each book in the series. Book introductions and chapter prefaces are offered to provide background material for readers. Chapters are organized around several key questions that are answered with diverse opinions representing all points on the political spectrum. Materials in each chapter include opinions in which authors clearly disagree as well as alternative opinions in which authors may agree on a broader issue but disagree on the possible solutions. In this way, the content of each volume in Current Controversies mirrors the mosaic of opinions encountered in society. Readers will quickly realize that there are many viable answers to these complex issues. By questioning each author's conclusions, students and casual readers can begin to develop the critical thinking skills so important to evaluating opinionated material.

Current Controversies is also ideal for controlled research. Each anthology in the series is composed of primary sources taken from a wide gamut of informational categories including periodicals, newspapers, books, US and foreign government documents, and the publications of private and public organizations. Readers will find factual support for reports, debates, and research papers covering all areas of important issues. In addition, an annotated table of contents, an index, a book and periodical bibliography, and a list of organizations to contact are included in each book to expedite further research.

Perhaps more than ever before in history, people are confronted with diverse and contradictory information. During the Persian Gulf War, for example, the public was not only treated to minute-to-minute coverage of the war, it was also inundated with critiques of the coverage and countless analyses of the factors motivating US involvement. Being able to sort through the plethora of opinions accompanying today's major issues, and to draw one's own conclusions, can be a complicated and frustrating struggle. It is the editors' hope that Current Controversies will help readers with this struggle.

Introduction

"The true history of women in US politics is one of a slow and arduous fight for gender parity."

Women have made great progress in recent decades, racking up achievements in education, the workplace, government, and politics. However, according to the Center for American Women and Politics, women as of the end of 2011 still hold only ninety, or 16.8 percent, of the total seats in the 112th US Congress—seventeen of the 100 seats in the Senate and seventy-three of the 435 seats in the House of Representatives. The states of Delaware, Iowa, Mississippi, and Vermont have never elected a woman to either house of Congress. And no woman has ever been elected president or vice president of the United States. In fact, according to the WCF (Women's Campaign Forum) Foundation, the United States ranks ninetieth globally in terms of the number of women in national legislatures—below many less developed countries. The true history of women in US politics is one of a slow and arduous fight for gender parity.

The first significant milestone in US women's fight for political power was the 19th Amendment to the US Constitution, ratified by the states in 1920, giving women the right to vote. Although it is now difficult to believe, American women prior to this time were denied even this most basic political right. And acquiring voting rights for women was itself the result of a long and hard-fought struggle that began in July 1848, when the first women's rights convention was held in Seneca Falls, New York. There, Elizabeth Cady Stanton, an early women's rights advocate, wrote a Declaration of Sentiments stating that men and women are equal and setting forth a long list of grievances, including the fact that women were not permitted suffrage—that is, the right to vote. Later, advocates pushed for women to be granted voting rights along with African Americans when the nation adopted the 14th and 15th Amendments to the US Constitution (in 1868 and 1870, respectively), but in the end suffrage was given only to African Americans. This disappointment led women advocates such as Stanton—along with Susan B. Anthony, Lucy Stone, and others—to found various women's suffrage associations that in 1890 combined to form the National American Woman Suffrage Association (NAWSA). These right-to-vote supporters, called suffragists, brought court challenges, pushed for suffrage at the state levels, and introduced amendments to the federal Constitution year after year and decade after decade, never giving up. Finally, the US Congress mustered the two-thirds vote necessary to pass a women's suffrage amendment in May 1919, and the proposed 19th Amendment was sent to the states for ratification. Many southern states opposed the amendment, but it was ultimately ratified in July 1920. After much perseverance, women finally won the right to vote.

Following this victory, however, women still had a very limited role in politics for many more decades. As years went by, a few notable women were elected to the US Congress. One congresswoman was even elected three years before the right to vote was officially granted to women—Jeanette Rankin of Montana became the first woman member of the US House of Representatives in 1917. When Senator Thaddeus Caraway of Arkansas, died in office in 1931, his wife Hattie Caraway was appointed by the governor of Arkansas to take his seat. She won a special election in 1932, becoming the first woman to be elected to the Senate, and went on to win the general election. In 1948, Margaret Chase Smith of Maine was elected to the US Senate and made history as the first woman to serve in both houses of Congress. The advent of the modern women's feminist movement in the 1960s brought more strong female voices to the US Congress. In 1968, for example, Shirley Chisholm of New York became the first African-American woman elected to Congress. In 1970, the tenacious civil rights lawyer Bella Abzug, also of New York, took her place in the House of Representatives. And in 1976, Barbara Jordan, first elected to the US House of Representatives by Texas in 1972, became the first African-American woman to deliver a keynote speech at the Democratic National Convention.

Other milestones followed. In 1981, President Ronald Reagan appointed Sandra Day O'Connor as the first woman to serve on the US Supreme Court. A few years later, in 1984, Geraldine Ferraro, a representative from New York, was selected by Democratic presidential candidate Walter Mondale as the nations' first woman vice-presidential candidate of a major political party. More recently, in 2007, Representative Nancy Pelosi of California became the first woman Speaker of the US House of Representatives. And, of course, in 2008 Hillary Clinton almost succeeded in winning the Democratic nomination for the US presidency, but was beaten by Barack Obama.

Yet despite this history of firsts and steady progress in acquiring national and state elected positions, some commentators claim that women have yet to truly break the glass ceiling in US politics. The high point in terms of US Congress representation was 1992—dubbed by the media as "the Year of the Woman"—when twenty-four new women were elected to the US House of Representatives along with five new women who were elected to the US Senate. Never before had so many women been elected on the national stage, and many people thought this was the beginning of true political equality for women. Since then, women have continued to increase their numbers in both the Senate and the House of Representatives, from a total of thirty-two in 1992 to ninety today. Yet, as the percentage of women versus men in Congress reveals, this progress has been slow, and women still have a long way to go before they will be represented in equal numbers with men, compared with the overall US population.

The authors of the viewpoints included in *Current Controversies: Women in Politics* discuss the basic question of whether women have made substantial gains in US politics, along with other important issues, such as the status of women in world politics, whether women's participation improves politics, and what should be done to encourage more women to enter politics.

CHAPTER 1

Have Women Made Substantial Gains in US Politics?

Overview: Women in US Elective Office as of 2012

Center for American Women and Politics

The Center for American Women and Politics (CAWP)—part of the Eagleton Institute of Politics at Rutgers, The State University of New Jersey—is a research project that focuses on American women's political participation.

In 2012, 90 women serve in the U.S. Congress. Seventeen women serve in the Senate and 73 women serve in the House. The number of women in statewide elective executive posts is 72, while the proportion of women in state legislatures is 23.6 percent.

Congress

In 2012, women hold 90, or 16.8%, of the 535 seats in the 112th U.S. Congress—17, or 17.0%, of the 100 seats in the Senate and 73, or 16.8%, of the 435 seats in the House of Representatives. Congresswoman Nancy Pelosi (D-CA), who was the first woman Speaker of the House, is now minority leader.

Seventeen (12D, 5R) women serve in the Senate: Kelly Ayotte (R-NH), Barbara Boxer (D-CA); Maria Cantwell (D-WA); Susan Collins (R-ME); Dianne Feinstein (D-CA); Kirsten Gillibrand (D-NY); Kay Hagan (D-NC); Kay Bailey Hutchison (R-TX); Amy Klobuchar (D-MN); Mary Landrieu (D-LA); Claire McCaskill (D-MO); Barbara Mikulski (D-MD); Lisa Murkowski (R-AK); Patty Murray (D-WA); Jeanne Shaheen (D-NH); Olympia Snowe (R-ME); and Debbie Stabenow (D-MI).

"Fact Sheet: Women in Elective Office 2012," Center for American Women and Politics, 2012. www.cawp.rutgers.edu. Copyright 2012 Center for American Women and Politics. Reproduced by permission.

Seventy-three women from 27 states serve in the House of Representatives; 49 are Democrats and 24 are Republicans. In addition, three Democratic women serve as the Delegates to the House from Guam, the Virgin Islands and Washington, DC.

Since 1971, the number of women serving in state legislatures has more than quintupled.

Statewide Elective Executive Offices

In 2012, 74 women hold statewide elective executive offices across the country; women hold 23.3% of the 317 available positions. Among these women, 38 are Democrats, 35 are Republicans, and 1 was elected in a nonpartisan race.

GOVERNORS—6(2D, 4R)

AZ Jan Brewer (R)

NC Beverly M. Perdue (D)

NM Susana Martinez (R)

OK Mary Fallin (R)

SC Nikki Haley (R)

WA Christine Gregoire (D)

LIEUTENANT GOVERNORS—11 (4D, 7R)

AL Kay Ivey (R)

CT Nancy Wyman (D)

FL Jennifer Carroll (R)

IA Kim Reynolds (R)

IL Sheila Simon (D)

IN Becky Skillman (R)

MN Yvonne Solon (DFL)

NJ Kim Guadagno (R)

OH Mary Taylor (R)

RI Elizabeth Roberts (D)

WI Rebecca Kleefisch (R)

Attorney General—7 (5D, 2R)

Secretary of State—12 (8D, 4R)

State Treasurer/Chief Financial Officer—8 (6D, 2R)

State Comptroller—4 (1D, 3R)

State Auditor—6 (4D, 2R)

Chief State Education Official—5 (2D, 2R, 1 nonpartisan)
(*title varies from state to state*)

Agriculture and Commerce Commissioner—1R

Commissioner of Insurance—2 (1D, 1R)

Commissioner of Labor—1R

Corporation Commissioner—4(1D, 3R)

Public Service Commissioner—4 (3D, 1R)

Public Regulation Commissioner—1D

Public Utilities Commissioner—1R

Railroad Commissioner—1R

State Legislatures

In 2012, 1,747 (1,054D, 675R, 11 nonpartisan, 4 Progressive, 3 Independent), or 23.7%, of the 7,382 state legislators in the United States are women. Women hold 428 (264D, 152R, 11 nonpartisan, 1 Independent), or 21.7%, of the 1,971 state senate seats and 1,319 (790D, 532R, 4 Progressive, 2 Independent), or 24.4%, of the 5,411 state house seats. Since 1971, the number of women serving in state legislatures has more than quintupled.

As of January 2012, of the 252 mayors of U.S. cities with populations 100,000 and over, 44, or 17.6%, were women.

The states with the highest percentages of women state legislators are:

State	% Women
Colorado	40.0
Vermont	38.9
Hawaii	35.5
Arizona	33.3
Minnesota	32.3
Washington	32.0
Illinois	31.1
Maryland	30.9
Connecticut	29.9
New Jersey	29.2

Municipal Officials

As of January 2012, among the 100 largest cities in the U.S., 12 had women mayors. One is African American (Stephanie Rawlings-Blake, Baltimore); and one is Asian/Pacific Islander (Jean Quan, Oakland [Calif.]). In order of city population,[1] the mayors are:

City	Mayor	Rank
Houston, TX	Annise D. Parker	5
Fort Worth, TX	Betsy Price	17

---

1. According to data from the U.S. Bureau of the Census.

City	Mayor	Rank
Baltimore, MD	Stephanie Rawlings-Blake	24
Las Vegas, NV	Carolyn Goodman	31
Fresno, CA	Ashley Swearengin	35
Raleigh, NC	Nancy McFarlane	44
Oakland, CA	Jean Quan	48
Stockton, CA	Ann Johnston	68
Chula Vista, CA	Cheryl Cox	80
Glendale, AZ	Elaine M. Scruggs	91
N. Las Vegas, NV	Shari Buck	96
Irving, TX	Beth Van Duyne	97

As of January 2012, of the 252 mayors of U.S. cities with populations 100,000 and over, 44, or 17.6%, were women, including four African Americans, and one Asian/Pacific Islander. Of the 1248 mayors of U.S. cities with populations 30,000 and above, 217, or 17.4%, were women.[2]

Percentages of Women in Elective Offices

Year	US Congress	Statewide Elective	State Legislatures
1979	3%	11%	10%
1981	4%	11%	12%
1983	4%	11%	13%
1985	5%	14%	15%
1987	5%	14%	16%
1989	5%	14%	17%
1991	6%	18%	18%
1993	10.1%	22.2%	20.5%
1995	10.3%	25.9%	20.6%
1997	11.0%	25.4%	21.6%
1999	12.1%	27.6%	22.4%
2001	13.6%	27.6%	22.4%
2003	13.6%	26.0%	22.4%
2004	13.8%	26.0%	22.5%

2. Information was compiled using the United States Conference of Mayors' 2012 website directory, www.usmayors.org/uscm/meet_mayors, as the primary reference.

Year	US Congress	Statewide Elective	State Legislatures
2005	15.0%	25.7%	22.7%
2006	15.0%	25.1%	22.8%
2007	16.1%	24.1%	23.5%
2008	16.5%	23.2%	23.7%
2009	16.8%	22.6%	24.3%
2010	16.8%	22.5%	24.5%
2011	16.8%	22.1%	23.7%
2012	16.8%	23.3%	23.7%

The Burdens of Female Politicians

Monica Potts

Monica Potts is associate editor for The American Prospect.

In the nearly 30 years since Geraldine Ferraro was the first woman to grace a major party's presidential ticket, female politicians became less of a novelty. Ferraro's selection as Walter Mondale's vice-presidential candidate in 1984 was replicated by Sarah Palin on the Republican side in 2008, the same year Hillary Clinton almost became the Democratic nominee for the top spot. Pundits declared 1992, when more female senators were elected than ever before, "the year of the woman." And 31 women have served as governors since Ella Grasso became the first woman who wasn't the wife or widow of a politician to be elected governor—of Connecticut in 1974.

The world has changed since 1984, but not that much. We still haven't achieved the ultimate goal: parity in statehouses and Congress or sending a woman to the White House. Nor have we escaped the sexist prism through which women in politics are portrayed in the media and viewed by the public. But you do have women on the field, ranging from the exceedingly competent Hillary Clinton, who gets criticized for being too robotic, to the obviously incompetent Palin and Minnesota Rep. Michele Bachmann, who have ridden the coattails of the women's rights movement into office even as they undermine it at every turn.

Which puts feminists in a peculiar position. Of course neither Palin nor Bachmann is an obviously worse choice than all of their male peers (there is, after all, hardly a shortage of incompetent men in politics). But female office-holders bear a lot of weight—and withstand an inordinate amount of scrutiny—precisely because there are so few. And with so many expectations riding on them, they inevitably end up disappointing.

This was certainly the case with Ferraro. Until she was elevated to national prominence, Ferraro was an obscure Queens congresswoman. She became a prosecutor only after her children were older, and embraced the image of herself as a mother and homemaker. The Mondale campaign used that branding to preempt any criticism she might draw because of her gender. In addition, some of her policy positions—she opposed school busing and supported school vouchers, for example—put her at odds with the movement and with other progressive goals. But feminists were expected to vote for her anyway even though in fact, Ferraro was never as progressive as the party's selection of her was.

The female candidates who rose to prominence in 2012 are primarily conservative and don't support policies . . . that are important to most women.

If many of us weren't ambivalent about Ferraro before the 2008 presidential race, we certainly soured on her after. After saying Obama wouldn't have been the front-runner for the Democratic nomination if he were a white man, she responded to criticism by saying, "I really think they're attacking me because I'm white. How's that?"

But even more progressive female politicians tend to let everyone down. If Clinton was ferocious as a First Lady, she was decidedly less so as a candidate for president. She struggled to win over young, progressive female voters because she seemed too compromised, too conservative in many respects compared to Barack Obama. Rebecca Traister, a writer for *Salon* wrote in her excellent recount of the role of women in the election *Big Girls Don't Cry*, about the struggles feminists had with Clinton, who as the first serious contender for president should have had a lock on the feminist vote but did not. Of the period during which Clinton was the front-runner in the 2008 Democratic race, she wrote, "One of the strangest things about this moment, for which Clinton would pay dearly, was that when her victory was presumptive many American feminists did not cheer her on, but shrugged their shoulders, curled their lips in distaste, or simply kept their distance."

Clinton—whose tenure as secretary of state is both remarkable and mostly unremarked upon—will likely leave politics, at least in an official capacity, at the end of Obama's first term. And the women we're left with after Clinton are even worse. The female candidates who rose to prominence in 2012 are primarily conservative and don't support policies like equal pay and access to abortion and reproductive health that are important to most women—and prerequisites for anyone who identifies as a feminist.

Bachmann has thrown her hat into the ring from the right for 2012, but Palin, once thought a top contender, isn't running for certain. At first, Palin seemed uniquely able to balance sex appeal and careerism—her dual roles as mother and politico—in a way that few female politicians ever do. But the more the media focused on her, the more she looked ridiculous and was pushed out of the front-runner spot whether she deserved it any less than her male colleagues or not.

This is not to say that Palin should have been given a pass despite her obvious lack of knowledge of world affairs; it's to say that the presence of women like Bachmann and Palin in the spotlight isn't the problem per se. Most women would likely be thrilled to have a whole range of female candidates to choose from, but for that to happen, there need to be more of them. Only then will female candidates no longer have to shoulder the burden of representing an entire class, and only then will feminists not have to hang their hopes on a single candidate. Ferraro was an imperfect candidate—and a disappointment to progressives in many ways—but one has to hope that the burdens she had to bear will be buried with her.

Hillary Clinton's Run for President Had a Positive Effect on US Politics

Jessica Valenti

Jessica Valenti is a writer and the founder of Feministing.com, a feminist blog site.

It's official. Americans won't be inaugurating a woman president next January [2009]. From a feminist perspective it's hard not to feel a bit defeated. Even for those who, like me, preferred Barack Obama, there's still that chilling feeling that maybe sexism scored a point this campaign season. But even though Hillary Clinton's candidacy is at an end, the effect it has had on women and politics is reason enough for feminists to chin up.

Hillary Clinton's Positive Effects

For perhaps the first time ever there has been a national conversation about women's political participation—much of it among women. Dana Goldstein at the *American Prospect* wrote this week: "Over the course of this historic, thrilling, aggressive primary election, we've seen more female pundits than ever before writing and speaking about presidential politics ... [and] experienced unprecedented interest from male politicos in women's participation in the electoral process."

Clinton's run is also sure to have a lasting effect on women considering running for office. Marie Wilson, president and founder of The White House Project, noted: "More young women ... are motivated because they have seen her persist."

Jessica Valenti, "Hillary's Loss Can Still Be a Gain for American Women," *The Guardian*, June 6, 2008. www.guardian.co.uk. Copyright © 2008 by Guardian News & Media Ltd. Reproduced by permission.

There's even a silver lining to be found in the distressing downsides of her candidacy. As someone who spots sexism for a living, I found myself absolutely shocked at the amount of gender-based vitriol directed at Clinton. But while the unrelenting sexism in the media coverage of Clinton's campaign was a harsh reminder of how pervasive misogyny is in America, we needed that reminder.

For the feminist movement itself, the benefits of Clinton's candidacy may have to be worked for.

I'd like to think the sheer volume of public misogyny jump-started a nation-wide dialogue about sexism. Because every time a pundit called Clinton's voice "grating", someone at home watching television cringed. When several young men at a campaign stop in New Hampshire thought it would be just hilarious to yell out "Iron my shirt!," there was public outrage. And when MSNBC host Chris Matthews asked former Democratic presidential candidate Chris Dodd if he "found it difficult to debate a woman", he was roundly mocked in the political blogosphere. (Even by Dodd himself, who looked at Matthews curiously before answering: "No, not at all.")

Though sexist pundits and misogynists-for-fun weren't held nearly accountable enough, it's heartening to know that now there can be no denying that yes, Virginia, there is sexism.

Feminist Concerns

For the feminist movement itself, the benefits of Clinton's candidacy may have to be worked for. The election put a brutal spotlight on an undeniable divide between feminists, largely the result of an already-brewing generational tension.

A *New York Times* opinion piece by Gloria Steinem that claimed sexism was a bigger problem in America than racism, and a widely circulated article by Robin Morgan suggesting young women voting for [Barack] Obama were "eager to win male approval", set the stage for a battle that left many disenchanted. After all, why was the only "appropriate" feminist vote one for Clinton? And the assumption that younger women who supported Obama were simply being naive or—even more insulting—voting to please their boyfriends, didn't exactly sit well.

> *Clinton's campaign didn't need to be successful for it to mean something incredibly important for American women.*

Feminists of all ages also resented how the mainstream movement seemed to be pitting sexism against racism in their campaign conversations. Latoya Peterson of the popular blog *Racialicious.com* wrote: "While I can truly understand if some women feel that their gender problems take more prominence than their race problems, other women need to understand that, for some of us, that separation does not happen. Our discrimination is not race neutral. So why should our feminism be?"

Generational divides and concerns that mainstream feminism focuses its energy on white women, above all others, are not new. But now that they're out in the open being discussed, we have an amazing opportunity to fight for an even-better women's movement.

Martin Luther King, in his "Letter from a Birmingham Jail", noted: "We merely bring to the surface the hidden tension that is already alive. We bring it out in the open, where it can be seen and dealt with. Like a boil that can never be cured so long as it is covered up but must be opened with all its ugliness to the natural medicines of air and light, injustice must be exposed, with all the tension its exposure creates, to the light of human conscience and the air of national opinion before it can be cured."

Clinton's campaign didn't need to be successful for it to mean something incredibly important for American women. Whether it's uncovering the ugly boil of American sexism or a battling for a better feminist movement, a new conversation has been started about women and political power. And now that we're here, with our wounds uncovered, we're tending to them with an eye towards the future.

Women Made Modest Gains in the 2008 US Elections

Linda Feldmann

Linda Feldmann is a staff writer for The Christian Science Monitor.

For women in politics, 2008 was both an extraordinary and an ordinary year. The extraordinary—the candidacies of Hillary Rodham Clinton and Sarah Palin for national office—dominated headlines and sparked national discussions about gender and power.

Business as Usual

But even as the highest glass ceiling in American politics came the closest it ever has to being shattered, in Congress it was business as usual: Women made a net gain of one seat in the Senate, bringing the total to 17 out of 100, and three seats in the House, moving up from 71 to 74 out of 435 seats, or 17 percent. At least the numbers keep going up, say advocates for women in politics, but the United States still lags woefully in world rankings.

As of Oct. 31 [2008], the US ranked 71st out of 188 countries for its percentage of women in the lower House, according to the Inter-Parliamentary Union.

"At this rate, it will take us till 2063 to reach parity," says Marie Wilson, president of the White House Project, an organization working to advance women in leadership. "I mean, come on! We have to speed things up."

Linda Feldmann, "Women Make Modest Gains in Election 2008," *The Christian Science Monitor*, November 16, 2008. csmonitor.com. Copyright © 2008 The Christian Science Publishing Society. All rights reserved. Reproduced by permission from Christian Science Monitor, (www.csmonitor.com).

Bright Spots

At the state level, the pipeline into federal office, there were some bright spots in 2008: A record number of women, 2,328, ran for state legislatures in a presidential election year, surpassing the previous presidential-year record of 2,302 set in 1992. (The overall record was set in 2006, when 2,429 women ran. More state legislative seats are up for election in non-presidential election years.)

"So 2008 was a record, and it managed to get us from 23.7 percent of women serving in state legislatures to 24.2 percent," says Debbie Walsh, director of the Center for American Women and Politics at Rutgers University in New Brunswick, New Jersey.

Women's advocates are hopeful that the examples of Senator Clinton and Governor Palin will spur more women, of all political stripes, to throw their hats in the ring.

Another bright spot emerged in New Hampshire, where women now hold a majority in the state Senate, 13 out of 24 seats—the first state legislative body in US history to be majority female. New Hampshire, and New England in general, has a history of electing women to office, owing to a tradition of citizen part-time legislators. In New Hampshire, the annual pay for legislators is $100, plus travel reimbursement.

Overall, when the totals of each state's legislative bodies are combined, Colorado ranks No. 1 for female representation, with 38 percent. Vermont has 37.8 percent, and New Hampshire, 37.7 percent.

"Once we drop the decimal points, we know that women will have arrived," writes former Vermont Gov. Madeleine Kunin in a blog. In an interview, she notes that the citizen-legislator model of her state is what allowed her to get into politics when her four children were young. In contrast, South Carolina now has no women in its state senate.

Hope for the Future

Women's advocates are hopeful that the examples of Senator Clinton and Governor Palin will spur more women, of all political stripes, to throw their hats in the ring. Both demonstrated how far one can go, even without the typical resume for high office. Clinton lacked executive experience and Palin had less than two years as governor of Alaska. . . .

Did the Clinton and Palin candidacies leave girls with a sense of possibility, or a feeling that you can run, but you can't win?

While women are inclined to wait to be asked to run for office, neither woman had to be invited. Palin had a particularly meteoric rise to national prominence, after taking on the Republican old-boys network of Alaska—a story that put her in Senator McCain's sights. In the end, come Inauguration Day in January [2009], it will be two men [Barack Obama and Joe Biden] taking the oath for the highest offices in the land. African-American parents can now point to President-elect Barack Obama as a role model for their kids.

But what about the parents of girls? Did the Clinton and Palin candidacies leave girls with a sense of possibility, or a feeling that you can run, but you can't win?

In *Monitor* interviews, young women and their mothers said they felt the 2008 election demonstrated that gender and race are not impediments to running as a credible candidate, and that even though a woman still has yet to be elected president, Mr. Obama's election helps pave the way for that to happen someday.

"Because Obama became the president, that's another possibility for us, because he is a minority, and women are considered a minority group in the social world," says Ashley Eden, a graduate student at the University of Central Florida in Orlando. "So I think that also is a benefit for women as well."

Her mother, Joni Eden, agrees. The election of Obama "gives our girls hope, but I think it gives everybody hope that they can . . . be anything they want to be."

"We say it all the time, but I don't think it's ever really been shown at this level," adds Ms. Eden, an executive assistant at Rollins College in Winter Park, Fla.

The legions of young women who volunteered for the Obama campaign—to the frustration of Clinton supporters—are a testament to the sense of younger women these days that they feel empowered enough that they don't have to vote their gender.

Advocates of women in politics hope that all these young women who volunteered, both Democrat and Republican, will turn that activism into running for office themselves someday.

"Definitely, I think that young girls know that women can go far," says Katya Ruiz, a high school junior in suburban Orlando. "It's not a question of knowing that. We know that. And I think we're very empowered now."

Her mother, Margarita Koblasz, an instructor in legal studies at the University of Central Florida, adds to the thought: "[That's] different from the generation that we grew up in and different from the generation that our mothers grew up in. . . . Now I've got a daughter saying of course women can be president, which wasn't something we could be taught."

Women's Political Gains Have Increased Women's Economic Power

Carolyn Maloney

Carolyn Maloney is a US congresswomen from the state of New York.

O ver 25 years ago [in July 1984], Geraldine Ferraro was nominated as the Democratic Party's Vice Presidential candidate, shattering the political glass ceiling and ushering in a new era of political leadership for women.

As the first female Chair of the U.S. Congress Joint Economic Committee, I wanted to know if women's political gains have translated into economic gains for women. A report released this week by the Joint Economic Committee, "Women and the Economy 2010: 25 Years of Progress But Challenges Remain," confirms the concurrent economic strength of women as they have gained political power.

Progress and Challenges

The report is a tale of progress, but also one of challenges. Women work more, earn more, and are more educated today than they were 25 years ago. Yet, women, and in particular working mothers, run up against a stubborn pay gap, continued barriers to employment in key sectors of the economy, and persistent tension between work and family responsibilities.

The report finds that working women's incomes play an increasingly critical role in the economic well-being of families. Families depend on women's earnings to pay for housing, clothing, groceries, and children's college education. Two facts

Carolyn Maloney, "Translating Women's Political Gains into Economic Power," *The Huffington Post*, August 26, 2010. www.huffingtonpost. Reproduced by permission.

from the report clearly illustrate just how central women's earnings have become over the past 25 years to many families' economic bottom line.

- In 1983, wives' incomes comprised just 29 percent of total family income. But by 2008, wives' incomes represented 36 percent of total family income.

- Between 1983 and 2008, married couples with a working wife experienced average annual income growth of 1.12 percent, while married couples with a stay-at-home wife saw their average annual incomes decline by 0.22 percent per year.

The report also points out that challenges remain if women are to be stronger contributors to America's economic progress. While more women are working and women now make up nearly half of the workforce, a significant gender wage gap still persists. The average full-time working woman only earns 80 cents for every dollar earned by the average full-time working man.

While we have come a long way, there is still more work to be done to achieve equality in the workplace so that the economic power behind half of our labor force is fully unleashed.

And women are still significantly underrepresented in certain sectors of the economy that provide good jobs without a college degree, like manufacturing and construction.

More Work to Do

Democrats in Congress have worked for legislation that acknowledges the challenges that women still face in the workplace and seeks to improve their ability to meet these challenges. I am proud that the first piece of legislation that

President [Barack] Obama signed into law was the Lilly Ledbetter Fair Pay Act, which gave women the right to challenge illegal wage discrimination. But our efforts have not stopped there. Democratic women have continued the legacy of Geraldine Ferraro and have shaped policies that are central to women's economic well-being including family and medical leave, child care, health care, and equal pay.

American women have shown the world that change can happen. And today, with a growing share of women working, and women earning a growing share of their families' income, women stand poised to be the engine of economic growth as the United States recovers from the Great Recession.

Today [August 26, 2010] we celebrate the 90th anniversary of women's right to vote and pay tribute to those women whose votes both in the ballot box and in our legislative chambers have created economic opportunities for all Americans. While we have come a long way, there is still more work to be done to achieve equality in the workplace so that the economic power behind half of our labor force is fully unleashed.

Fewer Women Are Seeking Elective Office

Kate Linthicum

Kate Linthicum is a reporter for the Los Angeles Times.

Fifteen people sit on the Los Angeles City Council. It's possible that in a few months, only one will be a woman. In a few years, there could be none.

If City Councilwoman Janice Hahn wins a July [2011] runoff election for a South Bay congressional seat, Jan Perry will be the council's lone female. And Perry must surrender her seat in 2013 because of term limits. [Hahn won the special election on July 12, 2011.]

Eleven years ago, a third of the desks lining the council chamber's ornate horseshoe were filled by women. The steady decline reflects a broader trend across the nation, where the proportion of women officeholders has been flat-lining or slipping.

Women's Representation in Politics Dropping

The number of women sworn in to Congress this year [2011] fell for the first time in 30 years, leaving women with just 16% of congressional seats.

And the number of female lawmakers in state capitals decreased by 81 this year, the largest percentage drop in decades.

The prominence of women like Secretary of State Hillary Clinton and former Alaska Gov. Sarah Palin on the national stage may give a false impression of the political influence women wield and ease pressure on women to run for office.

That could be especially true in California, where both United States senators, several members of Congress, the attorney general and secretary of state are women.

"I think that the average person could get fooled into thinking we have more representation than we actually do," said Katherine Spillar, vice president of Feminist Majority, an organization that promotes equality for women.

The once-rapid growth in women tossing their hats into the ring has stalled.

Spillar said that even in this era of post-identity politics, women's representation in politics at the national and local level is critical.

"Women are often more acutely aware of needs in the education system, and they have a different understanding on needs in healthcare, transportation," she said. "Having those perspectives represented when tens of millions of dollars of a city budget are being allocated, that matters."

Women Are Not Running for Office

So what changed since 1992's "Year of the Woman," when females gained 22 seats in Congress?

For one, the once-rapid growth in women tossing their hats into the ring has stalled.

"When women run, women win at the same rate as men in comparable elections," said Debbie Walsh, director of the Center for American Women and Politics at Rutgers University. "But they haven't been running."

No one can say for sure why, but political scientists suspect one cause is the ever-increasing opportunities for well-educated women in business. Others may be the coarseness permeating many campaigns, and the reputation of politics as a man's world.

In the past, some women saw the Los Angeles City Council as an inhospitable place.

In 1995, then-City Councilwoman Laura Chick made headlines when she called the council the "most sexist, good-old-boys work environment that I've ever been in."

Chick, who in 2001 became city controller and thus the first woman elected to a citywide office, told reporters that some of her council colleagues made off-color jokes and sexually suggestive comments during meetings.

The tenor of modern campaigning, with its frequent intrusions into family and personal life, may discourage women [from entering politics.]

Problems in Los Angeles

For whatever reasons, the decline of female candidates appears especially acute in Los Angeles, according to Bettina Duval, founder of California List, which identifies potential women candidates for statewide office and helps them get elected.

So far, no female candidates have emerged as potential contenders for Hahn's City Council seat, a prospect Duval called "stunning."

Three men, former Councilman Rudy Svorinich, Assemblyman Warren Furutani (D-Gardena) and Pat McOsker, president of the United Firefighters of Los Angeles City, have signaled interest in representing Hahn's Watts-to-San Pedro district.

The tenor of modern campaigning, with its frequent intrusions into family and personal life, may discourage women, Perry said. "I can only imagine that some women don't go into politics because they see that it's such a nasty process."

She said she was so disturbed by the possibility of a City Council with no women that she has been looking for a woman to replace herself and begun grooming a possible successor.

"Women bring different perspectives," she said, noting that it was councilwomen who fought for equal pay for female city workers in the 1990s.

Perry, who worked as a council aide to former Councilwoman Rita Walters during that time, said the gender dynamics of the panel have changed for the better in recent years, in part because term limits ushered in a new crop of lawmakers.

The leap to a political career can pose different challenges for women.

The "culture of sexism from the 1990s and before is long gone," said City Council President Eric Garcetti.

"But it's more than getting rid of the culture of sexism," he said. "It's making sure there is representation. We need a council that looks like Los Angeles."

Other groups also are underrepresented on the council. For example, only one Asian American has ever served: Michael Woo, who represented Garcetti's 13th District.

There are many women in key City Hall roles: department managers, legislative analysts, the top ranks of council staff. But the leap to a political career can pose different challenges for women.

Wendy Greuel was single when she successfully ran for City Council at age 40. Her mother was supportive but warned she would never find a husband or have children if she won.

Greuel, now city controller, met her future husband at a campaign stop and had a son, Thomas, not long after entering office. A nanny would take him to City Hall each day, and Greuel would run to her office to nurse him during meeting breaks.

She said she sometimes felt more scrutinized than her male colleagues who were parents. At one community event, she said, she was heckled and told to go home and "be a real mom to your child."

Greuel, a possible mayoral candidate, said that being a mother gave her a unique perspective on some issues, such as education. But she rejected the idea that she should focus on "women's issues." She chaired the transportation committee and was the vice chairwoman of the powerful budget and finance committee.

Guys don't need to be recruited. Women usually do.

Former City Councilwoman Jackie Goldberg said every issue is a women's issue. "Women bring a different perspective even to the things that everybody agrees we should be talking about," she said.

She recalled council discussions of the merits of publically funded after-school programs. The councilmen, she said, thought about them in terms of gang prevention. But the councilwomen considered the broader effects on families.

Goldberg, who started her political career at age 38, when she ran for the Los Angeles Unified School District's Board of Education, noted that women who run for office often do so at a later age than men. Part of the reason, she said, is that they're often busy raising families.

"Most men in office who have kids are not the primary caregivers," she said. "Guys don't need to be recruited. Women usually do."

About once a month, Goldberg says, someone calls seeking her advice about running for office.

"I've yet to have a woman call," she said.

The 2010 Midterm Congressional Elections Produced a Historic Decrease in the Number of Women in the US Congress

Meghan Smith

Meghan Smith is the managing editor of The Gavel, *a newspaper published by Boston College.*

Despite the fact that many women ran in the primaries for the 2010 midterm elections, when the 112th Congress is sworn in this January [2011], there will be a decline in the number of female members in Congress.

A Historic Decrease in Female Representation

Women in the next US Congress are projected to make up just 16 percent of the members, down from 17 percent in the previous Congress. Although the actual number of seats lost is not a huge number, the change is still significant because it is the first decrease that women in Congress have seen in 30 years.

Although the number of women in Congress has never been close to proportional to that of the American population, for the past three decades each Congress has seen a steady increase in the number of women holding seats in the Senate and House of Representatives. This trend began in 1978, and women have slowly made progress in each succeeding election.

Meghan Smith, "Number of Women in Congress Faces Historic Decline," *The Gavel* online, December 10, 2010. bcgavel.com. © 2010 Gavel Media, Inc. Reproduced by permission.

The [2010] election cycle started out looking promising for women, with more female candidates seeking nominations than ever before. During the primaries, 262 women ran for House seats, which marks an increase from the previous record of 222 set in 1992, a year that was called the "Year of the Women." Of the 113 female Republican candidates who challenged incumbents, only 32 were successful. Of the 80 Democratic women who challenged incumbents, 37 were elected.

The US is far behind other countries with respect to female representation in governing institutions.

Although female Republican candidates like Meg Whitman [who ran for governor of California], Carly Fiorina [who ran for US Senate in California], Christine O'Donnell [who ran for US Senate in Delaware] and Sharron Angle [who ran for US Senate in Nevada] drew a lot of attention in the general election, they lost in their respective races. The Tea Party played a big role in many elections in this cycle.

Boston College professor Abigail Brooks, who teaches sociology and women's studies, said that a possible reason for the decrease of women in Congress this year can be attributed to the general anger against the Democrats. She said in an email, "I might also hypothesize that since, in this election cycle, there was a backlash against the Democratic party and the progressive policies the party advocates, that there would be a corresponding backlash or decline in women's representation in politics," Brooks said. "Since, despite some recent high-profile Republican female candidates, generally speaking, the majority of women running, and currently holding, political office in the United States are Democrats."

Although recent, visible female politicians like Secretary of State Hillary Clinton, House Speaker Nancy Pelosi and former Vice Presidential candidate Sarah Palin are remaining very active in American politics, the US is far behind other countries with respect to female representation in governing institutions. According to a report from the Inter-Parliamentary Union, the US ranks 90th in the percentage of women represented in the country's houses of government. This is also due to the fact that many countries have certain quotas that need to be filled so that a proportional number of women can be elected.

Not only will the number of women in Congress decrease, but many of the female members of Congress will also lose their leadership roles. Since the Republicans will have a majority in the House, they will take control of leadership and committee positions.

The lack of female leaders in our current society, especially in politics, can be attributed to the difficulty that many women face because of stereotypes in our culture.

The most notable change will be that of Democrat Nancy Pelosi, the current Speaker of the House and the first woman to hold the position. This position will go to John Boehner, who is the current Republican House Minority Leader. Three women who are currently chairwomen of committees will also lose their seats. These include Rep. Louise Slaughter of the House Rules Committee, Rep. Nydia Velazquez of the Small Business Committee and Rep. Zoe Lofgren of the House Ethics Committee.

The change of leadership in the Senate will not change as drastically since the Democrats will still hold the majority. The most notable leadership change for female Senators will be Senator Blanche Lincoln of Arkansas, who is currently chairwoman of the Agriculture Committee and lost her re-election race in November. There will still be three female committee chairwomen, Sen. Dianne Feinstein on the Intelligence Committee, Sen. Barbara Boxer on the Environment and Public Works Committee and Sen. Mary Landrieu on the Small Business Committee, all of whom are Democrats.

Gender Stereotypes

According to Brooks, the lack of female leaders in our current society, especially in politics, can be attributed to the difficulty that many women face because of stereotypes in our culture.

"It continues to be somewhat difficult for many Americans to conceive of a female president because of deeply embedded, and I would argue socially and culturally constructed, beliefs about women's characteristics—overly emotional, a lack of intelligence and rationality, a lack of toughness and strength—as distinct from men's," Brooks said.

It is still unclear how this more conservative Congress will govern differently. Brooks said that it could mean there will be less attention paid to issues that affect women.

"Having less women represented in politics also means less attention, awareness, and policy work focused on aspects that effect women disproportionately such as affordable, quality childcare, maternity and paternity leave, reproductive rights, violence against women, the wage gap, among other issues," Brooks said.

Despite the loss in Congress, women made considerable progress in gubernatorial races.

Some female members of Congress have voiced concern that the number of women is considerably low. Senator Susan Collins, a Republican from Maine, told CNN, "It does concern me that there are not more women in leadership positions. That I do think is disappointing."

Representative Cathy McMorris Rodgers of Washington has said that women in leadership positions are an important part of Congress.

"It is an important voice that is heard at the table and it's a little different perspective than the men bring," McMorris Rodgers told CNN. "It's important that we are reflecting America."

Despite the loss in Congress, women made considerable progress in gubernatorial races. Three states elected their first female governors: Susana Martinez in New Mexico, who is also the first Latina governor in the US, Nikki Haley in South Carolina, and Mary Fallin in Oklahoma. All three of these women are Republicans.

"It traditionally has been more difficult for women to break the executive glass ceiling than the legislative glass ceiling," Collins said. "It is highly significant."

Women Have a Long Way to Go to Reach Parity with Men in Congress

Nicholas Kusnetz

Nicholas Kusnetz is a journalist based in New York City whose work has appeared in major newspapers and other publications.

As an early start to the 2010 election cycle, January's [2010] special election in Massachusetts briefly brought gender into mainstream political discussion. Yes, Scott Brown ran a strong campaign, capitalized on the ire of independent voters and generally outmaneuvered Martha Coakley to secure a comfortable upset victory in the U.S. Senate race, all in ways that had little to do with their genders.

But it was hard to ignore the fact that Coakley is a woman and that Massachusetts has a sad history of electing women to public office.

That contest doesn't necessarily forecast anything in races across the country in various primaries this spring or in November, but it was a reminder of how far we still have to go to approach parity for men and women in American politics. While women candidates may take advantage of voters' desire for change, it's unlikely the balance of congresswomen to men—women make up 17 percent of Congress, with that number having risen only three points over the last decade—will change dramatically this November.

In California, for example, where voters vote Tuesday [June 8, 2010] in party primaries, the Republicans have strong women candidates seeking the GOP [Republican] nomination for governor and U.S. Senate. But should former Hewlett-Packard CEO Carly Fiorina win her party's nod, she'll almost

Nicholas Kusnetz, "Stagnating Gains for Women in Politics," Miller-McCune.com, June 7, 2010. Copyright © 2010 Miller-McCune Inc. Reproduced by permission.

certainly face incumbent Barbara Boxer in the final vote. [Fiorina won the GOP nomination and was defeated by Boxer.]

Getting Women to Run

An early count by the Center for American Women and Politics lists 216 potential women running in the House [of Representatives] and 23 in the Senate. Those levels are largely consistent with numbers throughout the last 20 years. The best year for women candidates in both chambers of Congress was 1992 when 251 ran.

The question some advocates are asking is, how do we get more women to run?

Not surprisingly, it is this number—how many women run for office—that is most important, as women and men win races at the same rate. In 1992, women candidates saw opportunity to run as outsiders after the savings and loan crisis, the hearings for Clarence Thomas' nomination to the Supreme Court, and other scandals, said Jennifer Lawless, director of the Women & Politics Institute at American University. But despite both 2008 and the upcoming elections seeming to offer similar chances, we're not seeing the same result.

"The problem is that women are not running at the rates we'd expect them to given the credentials they have," Lawless said.

So the question some advocates are asking is, how do we get more women to run?

To try to answer that, Sheila Capone-Wulsin and Swanee Hunt are starting the Political Parity Project, which seeks to have more women running in gubernatorial and Congressional races.

"It comes out of the 2008 elections, which were incredibly energizing," said Capone-Wulsin, who used to run the Massachusetts Women's Political Caucus. "And yet women really made no gains."

Obstacles for Women Candidates

The central obstacle to getting more women in elected office is the fact that they are less likely to even want to run for office. The difference in media treatment of the two candidates in Massachusetts showed exactly why that's the case, said Hunt, who has been advocating to get more women in politics for decades.

People who study women in politics say voters tend to see women as agents of change, a fact that could help candidates in an election when approval of Congress is at record lows.

"During the campaign, Martha Coakley was condescendingly referred to as an 'ice queen' and a 'babe,'" Hunt wrote in an e-mail, "yet Scott Brown's nude photo in Cosmopolitan was barely mentioned. This media bias needs to be addressed."

Research has shown that women are less likely to think of themselves as qualified to run and less willing to go through the campaign process, and the researchers attributed this partly to media coverage. Furthermore, these attitudes and differences have changed little in recent years.

Despite the stagnating gains of women in elected office, both Hunt and Capone-Wulsin remain optimistic about November and are looking to a number of open seats where women are running, including seven in the Senate and 20 in the House. Though it is difficult to link gender stereotypes to voting patterns, people who study women in politics say voters tend to see women as agents of change, a fact that could help candidates in an election when approval of Congress is at record lows. Hunt thinks women candidates may have their best shot by pointing out that it is predominantly men who have been running the show.

"Many attribute the economic downturn to the crisis in our financial industry and resent the multimillion-dollar bonuses given to bank employees even after the government bailout," Hunt said. "When Congress held hearings with the heads of those large financial institutions, all were represented by men. Women candidates can succeed with a message of change, accountability and transparency."

Another prominent advocate of women in American politics paints a less rosy picture. Celinda Lake, a pollster and expert on women voters who worked with the Coakley campaign in Massachusetts, was surprised by her findings on voter sentiment there.

"We were pretty startled in the electorate in Massachusetts how little appetite there was in electing a women," she said.

Lake is hesitant to apply what she found in Massachusetts to other races, but she's not optimistic. Her work suggests that women candidates often do not run well on economic issues and she worries that will hurt candidates in November.

The United States ranks 86th in the world in terms of representation of women in the national legislature, according to the Center for American Women and Politics, putting it behind Uganda, Spain and Cuba, to name a few. Politically turbulent years like this one offer an opportunity to improve, Lawless said, but only if more women start to run for office.

"If we don't have candidates that are going to jump at the opportunity," she said, "there won't be a change."

CHAPTER 2

What Is the Status of Women in World Politics?

Chapter Preface

Perhaps a sign of women's growing presence in world politics, three women involved in political work were awarded the 2011 Nobel Peace Prize—an international prize awarded annually by the Norwegian Nobel Committee for outstanding contributions promoting peace among nations. According to the Committee's announcement in October 2011, the three women chosen—Ellen Johnson Sirleaf, Leymah Gbowee, and Tawakkol Karman—will share the prize for "their non-violent struggle for the safety of women and for women's rights to full participation in peace-building work."[1] Only twelve women have been honored with this award in the history of the Nobel Peace Prize, compared with eighty-five men. In 2011, the amount awarded in the prize is about $1.45 million, so each of the three winners will receive about $483,000, along with a medal and a diploma.

One of the Nobel winners, Ellen Johnson Sirleaf, is president of Liberia, and the first woman to be democratically elected to lead a country in Africa. Since being inaugurated in 2006, she has worked to bring stability, peace, and economic development to Liberia after fourteen years of civil war that ravaged the country. According to her supporters, President Sirleaf has helped to improve education and health systems, create jobs, raise wages of civil servants, build roads and other infrastructure, and secure forgiveness of billions of dollars of Liberian debt.

However, even Sirleaf herself admits that progress has been less than what she had hoped for. Many Liberians are discouraged with her leadership and, in elections held on October 11, 2011, Sirleaf failed to win a second term as president by the required majority. Although international observers concluded that the election was fair, Sirleaf's opponent Winston Tubman claimed fraud and urged people not to vote again until things were sorted out. This resulted in an extremely low turnout for a runoff election between Sirleaf and Tubman on November 8, 2011. Nevertheless, Sirleaf won 90.2 percent of votes cast in the election and claimed victory, explaining that the election was legitimate and that she would reach out to all other presidential candidates and try to include them in her government.

A second Nobel winner, Leymah Gbowee also is from Liberia but holds no official government position. Instead, she is credited with mobilizing and becoming the voice of the Women of Liberia Mass Action for Peace—a peace movement started by women that brought about the end of civil war in Liberia in 2003. The movement began with women praying and singing in a local fish market and grew as thousands joined the cause. A documentary called *Pray the Devil Back to Hell* helped to publicize Gbowee's peace efforts around the world. Finally, ex-President Charles Taylor agreed to a meeting with the group, during which they demanded a ceasefire and peace talks that led to the Accra Peace Accord on June 17, 2003, in Accra, Ghana. Since the peace agreement, Gbowee has worked to improve the status of women in Liberia as a member of Liberia's Truth and Reconciliation Commission. She is now director of the Women in Peace and Security Network, a non-governmental organization that promotes peace, literacy, and political participation for women.

The third Nobel winner, Tawakkol Karman, emerged on the global scene as a leader of Yemen's peaceful protests against Yemen's authoritarian president Ali Abdullah Saleh—part of the so-called Arab Spring movement that has produced protests against oppressive governments throughout the Middle East. Often called the mother of Yemen's revolution, Karman is a 32-year-old journalist, human rights activist, and mother of three who had been protesting against the Saleh government for years. In January 2011 she was arrested and imprisoned by the ruling regime, and this action brought thousands of people to the streets to protest and call for her release. She was released the following day, but the incident helped to turn the public against Saleh and ignite the larger antigovernment protest movement.

Since then, Karman has continued to protest and speak out against the government, and in a deeply conservative Islamic country where women are rarely seen or heard, Karman has inspired tens of thousands of women to openly defy the ruling regime and participate in the Yemen protest movement. On November 23, 2011, after many months of violent protests, Saleh signed an agreement that effectively transferred his ruling power to his vice president, Abed Rabbo Mansour Hadi. The agreement allowed Saleh to retain his title until the presidential elections in February 2012.

Most commentators say, however, that the fact that Liberia and Yemen are continuing to experience political and social instability does not diminish the courage and leadership shown by the three Nobel winners in their struggles to confront oppression through peaceful means. Many people around the world hope that they can ultimately succeed in bringing long-term peace and prosperity to their respective countries. The viewpoints included in this chapter address the status of women in world politics.

Notes

1. "Nobel Peace Prize 2011," Nobelpeaceprize.org, October 7, 2011. http://nobelpeaceprize.org/en_GB/laureates/laureates-2011/announce-2011/.

Women Are Leaders of or Running for Office in the World's Largest Countries

Jenna Goudreau

Jenna Goudreau is a staff writer for Forbes.

On this year's [2011] *Forbes* list of the world's 100 most powerful women, three of the top five most powerful are politicians. There are eight heads of state, several new faces and almost every political returnee from last year's list moved up in the rankings. Why? "There cannot be true democracy unless women's voices are heard," [US Secretary of State] Hillary Rodham Clinton once famously said. More than ever, women are leading or running for office in many of the world's largest nations, demanding that representation inch closer to parity.

Women in Power Around the Globe

Women are taking up the highest offices around the globe. Ranked the No. 1 most powerful woman and female politician is German Chancellor Angela Merkel, who directly controls the $2.9 trillion GDP [gross domestic product, a measure of a country's total economic output] of Germany and influences the $14.8 trillion economy of the European Union [E.U.]. Germany is the world's fifth biggest economy and the largest nation led by a woman. In office since 2005, Merkel is now leading the charge to stabilize E.U. debt and keep the 17-member euro zone unified.

Just behind her at No. 2 on the list is U.S. Secretary of State Hillary Clinton, who is fourth in line to succeed the president. As the world ambassador of the largest single economy on earth, Clinton has advanced U.S. interests and policies overseas while pushing women's issues, development and education to the top of the foreign policy agenda. She is one of a handful of women to have run for U.S. president on a major ticket and undoubtedly paved the way for the women coming up in politics behind her.

In the U.S., women continue to break down barriers.

On the global playing field, Clinton may have even more status than her title conveys. Political commentator and fellow power woman Greta Van Susteren told *Forbes* recently, "She's different than most secretaries of state. When she lands in a country, [Clinton] might as well be the President of the United States. . . . The whole world knows her."

Ranked the third most powerful woman this year, Brazilian President Dilma Rousseff directs the world's eighth largest economy. Rousseff is the biggest mover on the list, climbing 92 spots to No. 3 in 2011 from No. 95 in 2010. When *Forbes* went to press last year [2010], she was ramping up for a run-off election in October that went in her favor, making Rousseff the first female head of government in Brazil. The economist and former Marxist guerrilla served previously as the country's Minister of Energy and Chief of Staff, during which a reported 24 million escaped absolute poverty. She's also embraced social media: her 750,000-plus followers landed her on our top-10 list of female power tweeters. Soon all eyes will be on Brazil as the nation gears up to host the 2014 World Cup and 2016 Olympics.

Other female world leaders like Sonia Gandhi, president of the Indian National Congress Party; Cristina Fernandez, president of Argentina; Julia Gillard, prime minister of Australia; Yingluck Shinawatra, prime minister of Thailand; Ellen Johnson-Sirleaf, president of Liberia; and Laura Chinchilla, president of Costa Rica, all prove that women are competent and capable government leaders—and that constituencies are ready and able to elect them.

Breaking Barriers in the United States

At home in the U.S., women continue to break down barriers. First Lady Michelle Obama does anything but sit idly in the White House, choosing instead to lead a forceful campaign against childhood obesity and swaying major corporations like Wal-Mart, PepsiCo and Kraft to join the cause. Plus, there is no longer one token woman in the president's cabinet; six women now hold cabinet or cabinet-level positions in the Obama administration, including Kathleen Sebelius, the secretary of Health and Human Services, and Janet Napolitano, the secretary of Homeland Security.

This year's press favorite is U.S. presidential candidate Michele Bachmann, the tough-talking, steely-eyed Minnesota congresswoman with sights set on the Oval Office. Likely taking a cue from former VP candidate Sarah Palin, Bachmann is another fiercely conservative "Mama Grizzly." She boasts of raising five children and 23 foster children—all teenage girls— and recently voted "no" to increasing the debt ceiling.

From the female chiefs of Germany and Brazil to the current cabinet members and presidential hopefuls of the U.S., women are beginning to own their political power around the globe.

According to a rough count made by nonprofit organization The White House Project, Bachmann is the ninth woman ever to run for president, a club that began in 1872 by Victoria Woodhull, who ran before women were legally able to vote. Of course, the U.S. has not yet nominated a female president and the proportion of women in lower offices remains shamefully uneven. Only 16.6% of Congress seats are filled by women, and just 8% of the nation's largest cities have female mayors.

One of the six female governors in America, Oklahoma Governor Mary Fallin recently told me the best way to move those numbers up is to get more women to run for office. "Women have typically been the decision-makers, and more women than men vote," she said. "We need to encourage women to *run*."

Beyond party affiliations, Clinton and Palin raised the profile of women in politics, and now Bachmann too will test assumptions about female leaders. Gov. Fallin, a friend of Bachmann's since they were the only two GOP [Republican] women in the freshman class of 2006, offered the praise: "Michele is a hard worker, a good debater and loves to rally the troops. Nothing backs her down." Fallin hasn't officially endorsed a candidate yet.

From the female chiefs of Germany and Brazil to the current cabinet members and presidential hopefuls of the U.S., women are beginning to own their political power around the globe. As Fallin notes, "Women keep marching forward."

Women Lag Behind Men in Political Power Even in the Developed World

Jesse Ellison

Jesse Ellison is a writer and editor who covers education, culture, and women's issues for Newsweek.

Just over a decade into the 21st century, women's progress can be seen—and celebrated—across a range of fields. They hold the highest political offices from Thailand to Brazil, Costa Rica to Australia. A woman holds the top spot at the International Monetary Fund; another won the Nobel Prize in economics. Self-made billionaires in Beijing, tech innovators in Silicon Valley, pioneering justices in Ghana—in these and countless other areas, women are leaving their mark.

But hold the applause. In Saudi Arabia, women aren't allowed to drive. In Pakistan, a thousand women die in honor killings every year. And in Somalia, 95 percent of women are subjected to genital mutilation. In the developed world, women lag behind men in pay and political power. The poverty rate among women in the U.S. rose to 14.5 percent last year, the highest in 17 years.

Women, Politics, and Political Stability

To measure the state of women's progress, *Newsweek* ranked 165 countries, looking at five areas that affect women's lives: treatment under the law, workforce participation, political power, and access to education and health care. Poring over data from the United Nations and the World Economic Forum, among others, and consulting with experts and academics, we measured 28 factors to come up with our rankings.

Jesse Ellison, "Where Women Are Winning," *The Daily Beast*, September 18, 2011. www.thedailybeast.com. Reproduced by permission.

Countries with the highest scores tend to be clustered in the West, where gender discrimination is against the law, and equal rights are constitutionally enshrined. But there were some surprises. Some otherwise high-ranking countries had relatively low scores for political representation and workplace clout. Canada ranked third overall but 26th in power, behind countries such as Cuba and Burundi. Does this suggest that a woman in a nation's top office translates to better lives for women in general? Not exactly. "Trying to quantify or measure the impact of women in politics is hard because in very few countries have there been enough women in politics to make a difference," says Anne-Marie Goetz, peace and security adviser for U.N. [United Nations] Women.

Economies flourish when women are included, in no small part because women reinvest some 90 percent of their income into communities and family.

Of course, no index can account for everything. Declaring that one country is better than another in the way that it treats more than half its citizens means relying on broad strokes and generalities. (The experience of a domestic servant can hardly be compared with that of an executive with an M.B.A. [masters degree in business administration], even if their citizenship is the same.) Some things simply can't be measured. (Is child care better or worse when provided by grandparents, or subsidized and mandated by government?) And cross-cultural comparisons can't account for differences of opinion. (Who's more oppressed: the girl in the miniskirt or the one in the hijab?)

Certain conclusions are nonetheless clear. For one thing, our index backs up a simple but profound statement made by Secretary of State Hillary Clinton last week [the week of September 12, 2011] at the Asia-Pacific Economic Cooperation summit, as she declared a tipping point for women. "When we liberate the economic potential of women, we elevate the economic performance of communities, nations, and the world," she said. "There is a stimulative and ripple effect that kicks in when women have greater access to jobs and the economic lives of our countries: Greater political stability. Fewer military conflicts. More food. More educational opportunity for children. By harnessing the economic potential of all women, we boost opportunity for all people."

With some states all but starting from scratch, tackling gender inequality may rank low on the list of priorities. But it shouldn't.

Indeed, the 20 countries that are best for women almost all have democratically elected governments and GDPs [gross domestic product, a measure of a country's total economic output] above $200 billion. Economies flourish when women are included, in no small part because women reinvest some 90 percent of their income into communities and family, compared with the less than 40 percent reinvested by men. The countries that ranked last are poor, in some cases ripped apart by war, and largely dependent on aid from the West. Afghanistan has one of the highest maternal mortality rates in the world. In Chad, where per capita income is just $164 a year and women need their husband's permission to open bank accounts, just 20 percent of adult women can read. No wonder, then, that global nonprofits are turning their attention to women and girls. At this week's Clinton Global Initiative, more than 50 new programs will be announced, including curbing sexual violence in Haiti and efforts to end child marriage.

In our own research, the country that holds some of the most significant lessons doesn't rank at the top or the bottom, although a decade ago, it almost surely would have come close to last. In 2003, after decades of civil war, Rwanda's transitional government passed legislation requiring that a third of the seats in Parliament be held by women. Today, its Parliament is more than 50 percent women, and girls are enrolled in secondary school at the same rate as boys. Last year the World Economic Forum ranked Rwanda first among East African nations in economic innovation.

There are lessons here for the Middle East as it emerges from the Arab Spring [the Arab rebellions that began in December 2010]. With some states all but starting from scratch, tackling gender inequality may rank low on the list of priorities. But it shouldn't. "The vibrancy of these potential democracies will depend on the participation of women," says Melanne Verveer, ambassador at large for global women's issues at the U.S. State Department. Or in Goetz's words, "Excluding women from postconflict recovery would be like trying to tie your shoes with one hand."

Women's Overall Gains in World Politics Are Uneven and Fragile

Melanne Verveer

Melanne Verveer serves as US ambassador-at-large for Global Women's Issues.

Women are half the world's population, yet hold less than one-fifth of the positions of power in national governments. While it is certainly true that women today have made tremendous gains in reaching the highest rungs of leadership—Brazil, Costa Rica, Kyrgyzstan, Liberia and Bangladesh are among the countries with female presidents—overall the gains remain uneven. Furthermore, the contributions women have made toward achieving peace, prosperity, governance, and civil society in many parts of the globe too often go unrecognized; their inclusion in the political processes of their countries remains limited.

Women as Forces for Change and Development

This week [June 30, 2011], coinciding with the Community of Democracies Ministerial in Vilnius, Lithuania, prominent female leaders representing government and civil society came together in a special conference to redress this imbalance and to commit to increasing support for women's participation in the public sphere. Co-chaired by President Dalia Grybauskaite of Lithuania and President Tarja Halonen of Finland, the "Women Enhancing Democracy: Best Practices" Conference underscores that women are central to building and sustaining

Melanne Verveer, "In Community of Democracies, Women Driving Political Change," *DipNote*, June 30, 2011. U.S. Department of State, Washington, DC.

democratic change everywhere. Representing the United States at the Community of Democracies Ministerial, [US] Secretary [of State] Hillary Clinton also joined us at the women's conference, energizing the participants with her inspiring words of encouragement in support of women working in the struggle for democracy and human rights.

> *Women's active engagement in politics, civil society, and government decision-making are key ingredients to building democracy.*

This timing of this conference is especially propitious given the essential role women are playing in the democratic movement sweeping across the Middle East and North Africa. Bringing together the women who experienced the collapse of the Soviet Union 20 years ago with women from Egypt, Tunisia, and across the Middle East who were on the frontlines of the Arab Spring [the Arab rebellions that began in December 2010], the conference illuminates the diverse yet instrumental ways women have been drivers of political, social and economic development. When women are empowered to fully participate in their country's political, economic and social spheres, and given the opportunity to work together, women can be force multipliers for democratic change, reform and economic growth. There is a mountain of data that positively correlates investment in women with a country's prosperity. Countries that fail to recognize the value of the female half of the population are short-changing their own development.

A Time for Vigilance

While there is much to be hopeful about, particularly given the enthusiasm and collective energy generated by the Vilnius gathering, we must remain vigilant. The horrific incidents of sexual violence being used to intimidate and punish protesters in the Middle East and North Africa, are a grim reminder that the rights of women are not fully protected and that many of the gains women have made are fragile at best. To address this collective concern, we also focused on the importance of strengthening women's social status and the need for greater leadership and accountability in tackling violence against women and human trafficking.

Democracy without women is a contradiction in terms.

Noting that democracy and economic prosperity go hand in hand, we also discussed the importance of women's economic advancement. The United States has been at the forefront in developing programs supporting women entrepreneurs to increase their economic independence, employment and earning potential. It was very beneficial to exchange experiences with other women who are also making inroads in this crucial area of women's advancement.

The women I met during the conference are a source of inspiration and strength and a testament to the need for more women in leadership and decision-making positions at all levels of society. We also need to seek ways to make it easier and more rewarding for girls to also aspire to enter the field of politics so their voices, energy and ideas can sustain a future generation of female leaders. Women's active engagement in politics, civil society, and government decision-making are key ingredients to building democracy.

Democracy without women is a contradiction in terms. Investing in women's political participation and encouraging women to seek leadership positions is investing in a future where democracy will truly take root and the benefits of peace, progress and prosperity are most likely to flourish.

Gender Issues Are Preventing Women from Making Greater Progress in World Politics

Farida Jalalzai and Mona Lena Krook

Farida Jalalzai is an assistant professor of political science at the Institute for Women's and Gender Studies at the University of Missouri-St. Louis. Mona Lena Krook is an assistant professor of political science at Washington University in St. Louis.

In recent times, the status of women in politics has captured the imagination of spectators around the world. In early 2008, much of this attention was focused on two women in particular: Hillary Rodham Clinton, the former First Lady running to become the first female president of the United States [and current US secretary of state], and Benazir Bhutto, the former prime minister of Pakistan assassinated following a campaign rally in December 2007. This follows on from interest in the election of other female leaders around the globe, like [Chancellor] Angela Merkel in Germany, [President] Michelle Bachelet in Chile, [President] Ellen Johnson-Sirleaf in Liberia, and [President] Pratibha Patil in India, and coincides with the election of record numbers of women to national parliaments worldwide. Such developments have sparked widespread discussion as to the role of sex and gender in political life. For some, the rise of several prominent female leaders reflects the important gains that women as a group have made in the political sphere. For others, however, the experiences and portrayals of female politicians, as well as the continued under-representation of women in politics more generally, draw attention to the many ways in which access to

Farida Jalalzai and Mona Lena Krook, "Beyond Hillary and Benazir: Women's Political Leadership Worldwide," *International Political Science Review*, Vol. 31, 2010. Copyright © 2010 by International Political Science Association. Reproduced by permission of SAGE Publications, Ltd. and the authors.

political office is still very much stratified by gender. These debates raise several questions: What is the status of women in politics today? What explains the increased election of women in some countries but not in others? Finally, what do these developments mean for women as a group?

In total, 71 women from 52 countries have joined the elite ranks of female national leaders between 1960 and 2009.

In this article, we address these questions by analyzing and comparing women in positions of executive and legislative leadership around the globe. Doing so requires that we first distinguish "sex" from "gender": while sex captures biological differences between women and men, gender refers to the social meanings given to these differences, which may vary both cross-culturally and over time. In most countries, norms of gender have traditionally prescribed distinct roles in society for the two sexes: men have been given primary responsibility for affairs in the public sphere, like politics and the economy, while women have been assigned a central position in the private sphere, namely the home and the family. Historically, the public-private divide served as an argument against women's right to vote, on the grounds that suffrage for women would disturb the balance between the public and private spheres. While it has been muted over time, this divide continues to manifest itself to the present day, albeit in different ways across cultural contexts, through elite and media scrutiny of the husbands and children of female aspirants, as well as largely unsubstantiated concerns about the broader "qualifications" of female candidates. As such, it is perhaps not surprising that women constitute a relatively small proportion of elected officials worldwide, at the same time that increases in their numbers may portend significant shifts in the gendered nature of the public sphere. . . .

Women as National Leaders

Historically, female national leaders have been rare. The first woman to enter a position of national leadership who was not a monarch was Sirimavo Bandaranaike, who became prime minister of Sri Lanka in 1960. Later in the same decade, two other prominent women, Indira Gandhi of India and Golda Meir of Israel, also rose to power as prime ministers. However, it was not until 1974 that Isabel Perón of Argentina became the first female president. In general, the progress in the early decades was slow: three women became national leaders in the 1960s, followed by six in the 1970s, and seven in the 1980s. In contrast, dramatic change began to occur in more recent decades: 26 women first obtained positions of top executive leadership in the 1990s, followed by 29 additional women through August 2009. In other words, the number of new female leaders nearly quadrupled between the 1980s and 1990s and this pattern was repeated again in the 2000s. As such, more than three-quarters of all female presidents and prime ministers have come to office in the years since 1990. These findings indicate that the growing number of women in executive posts is no illusion or artifact of media coverage; rather, more women are entering these positions than ever before.

In total, 71 women from 52 countries have joined the elite ranks of female national leaders between 1960 and 2009. This figure includes those women who have served on a temporary basis, for example as acting or interim leaders. However, it excludes those who have occupied positions that do not conform to presidential or prime ministerial office and in countries that are not politically autonomous. This overview reveals that these women in positions of executive leadership hail from geographically diverse locations. While the largest proportion is from Europe, other world regions also have large numbers of female leaders. Presently [in 2010], 16 of these women occupy political office: nine presidents and seven prime ministers. Together, they head countries in five regions: Asia, Africa, Europe, Latin America, and Oceania.

To date, most research on female national leaders has focused on the details of individual women's political careers. As such, comparative work on this topic is relatively sparse. Reviewing the literature, however, it is possible to make several observations with regard to these women's paths to power. What is perhaps most striking is that, contrary to many expectations, women have tended to become presidents and prime ministers in contexts where women's status lags far behind that of men in the educational and economic spheres, and in places where women face numerous constraints on their political and social participation. In fact, the only quantitative study on this topic finds a correlation between the presence of a female head of state or government and *lower* levels of parity of women to men in life expectancy, education, and income. Yet, at the same time, the women who accede to these positions are usually highly educated and considerably more privileged than women in the general population. Consequently, it is simplistic to assert that the education and economic status of women are not relevant to their political advancement. It is crucial for those who eventually rise to positions of national prominence, but this can be—and has been—achieved where women's overall status is low.

In general, women are more likely to serve in parliamentary systems and more often as prime ministers than as presidents.

Attempts to reconcile the paradox of female leaders in contexts in which women generally lack power have pointed to the importance of kinship ties as a path to office. Women's leadership in certain regions is largely limited to those with familial ties through marriage or blood connections to former executives or opposition leaders, many of whom were assassinated. In these cases, kinship ties are primary but gender continues to be salient to these women's election or appointment to office. There are compelling reasons why a woman may appear to be a more appropriate heir to political power. For example, a woman may not be seen as independently politically ambitious and therefore as easily pushed aside by male leaders after coming to office. Alternatively, because women are often viewed as unifiers of the family, they may be charged with the daunting task of uniting their country following a period of political conflict.

Providing unity is especially important given that a contributing factor to women's rule in many of these contexts is high levels of political instability and a lack of political institutionalization, benefiting select women in their pursuit of power. In some instances, independence causes various ethnic and religious factions suppressed during colonialism to become salient. This leads to frequent regime change, stemming from assassinations and repeated coups. These circumstances create more opportunities to gain access to executive posts than would normally be the case. The lack of institutional development that is associated with such turbulence allows for kinship, ethnicity, or charismatic leadership to play a greater role in politics, opening the way for some women to occupy leadership posts. Exactly how these patterns interact with political institutions, however, is not yet well understood.

At the same time, institutional features of the political system appear to be critical to women's executive advancement. In general, women are more likely to serve in parliamentary systems and more often as prime ministers than as presidents: there have been 40 female prime ministers and 31 female presidents. Some studies attribute the greater success of women in obtaining prime ministerial posts to their ability to bypass a potentially biased general public and be chosen by the party as parliamentary rules dictate. [Former Prime Minister] Margaret Thatcher of the United Kingdom and Angela Merkel of Germany are good examples of women rising to power through party promotion. This is different from the processes involved in becoming president within a presidential system, which typically relies on some sort of popular vote for ascension. Presidential and prime ministerial posts also differ in their authority, autonomy, and traits deemed necessary for success, all of which are shaped by notions of gender. More specifically, the fusion of executive and legislative authority within parliamentary systems features a prime minister who shares power with cabinet and party members. In these systems, collaboration is fundamental: the qualities necessary for successfully formulating programs are negotiation, collaboration, and deliberation, all typically considered more feminine. In contrast, presidents in presidential systems act independently of the legislature and generally are expected to lead in a quick and decisive manner, traits which are more often associated with masculinity.

Initially, research found that women's overall levels of education and labor force participation were closely correlated with levels of female parliamentary representation.

Women in National Parliaments

Women form a small minority of all parliamentarians worldwide. However, the current world average, 18 percent, is the highest proportion ever recorded. Attention to aggregate numbers nonetheless masks substantial variations across countries: while Rwanda and Sweden have nearly equal numbers of women and men in their national legislatures, others, such as Belize and Saudi Arabia, have no women at all. Early research on these variations noted that the countries with the most women in elected positions tended to be countries where women enjoyed a relatively high social and economic status and cultural norms supported women's political participation. Today, these patterns are less clear: while the countries in the world with the most women in politics in the late 1980s came from two recognizable groups, the Nordic region and the Communist bloc, those that top this list in the late 2000s include some of these same states but also a wide range of other countries in Africa, Europe, Latin America, and Oceania. In comparison, several countries with long democratic histories, as well as high scores on indicators of women's status, elect relatively few women, most notably the United Kingdom (19.5 percent), France (18.2 percent), and the United States (16.8 percent).

Comparative literature on this topic stretches back more than twenty years. It identifies three sets of factors shaping women's access to national legislatures. The first relates to political institutions. Scholars have found that countries with proportional representation (PR) electoral systems tend to have a much higher share of women in parliament than countries with majoritarian electoral arrangements. These disparities are explained by reference to the fact that PR systems often have higher district magnitudes, which open the way for women to be included as the total number of members per district increases, and closed party lists, which enable political parties to place women in electable positions on party slates. Combined, these factors appear to offer more opportunities for female candidates, because political parties may feel compelled to nominate at least a few women in order to balance their lists. These effects may be magnified by characteristics of political parties. The impact of district magnitude, for example, frequently depends upon party magnitude, or the number of seats that a party assumes that it will win in a particular district: parties expecting to win only a few seats are less likely to nominate women, while those that anticipate winning several seats are more likely to balance their tickets with some female candidates. Ideology also matters: left-wing parties tend to nominate more women than right-wing parties, stemming from differences in their support for traditional gender roles, as well as their willingness to take concrete steps to promote women to top positions on electoral lists.

Women . . . serve more often in systems where executive authority is more dispersed, as opposed to in those with more unified executive structures.

A second set of variables are social and economic. Initially, research found that women's overall levels of education and labor force participation were closely correlated with levels of female parliamentary representation. As such, women rarely achieved the higher socioeconomic status that forms the "eligibility pool" for elective office, because practices of sex segregation in most countries channel women into female-dominated, low-paying occupations such as nursing and education and men into male-dominated, high-paying occupations like law and management. These patterns are anticipated to be less prevalent in countries at higher levels of socioeconomic development, where processes of modernization enable women to gain access to education and the paid labor force, thus moving them into higher-status social and economic roles, which in turn can lead to greater influence in politics. However, other work has cast doubt on these findings, uncovering weak and sometimes even negative correlations between women's education and labor force participation and the proportion of women in elected office. Some account for this by suggesting that improvements in women's status may serve only as facilitating conditions. Others note that these factors may operate differently in developed versus developing countries: women's participation in the labor force, for example, appears to have a positive effect on women's representation in the former but no effect in the latter. Indeed, several developing countries have witnessed dramatic changes in the absence of these assumed developmental "prerequisites".

A third and final group of explanations focus on cultural factors. Studies of the Nordic countries attribute the relatively high proportion of women in parliament in this region to a political culture that places strong emphasis on social and economic equality. Other scholars explore the impact of religion and find that Christian countries tend to have more women than countries with other dominant religions. These effects stem from the ways in which religion may intersect with cultural prohibitions on women's political activity, forbidding women from speaking in front of men, seeking political office, or attending political meetings. These norms, of course, are rooted in the public-private divide, which plays a major role in socializing women and men into prescribed gender roles, calling into question the legitimacy of women's political engagement and conferring private sphere responsibilities on women that prevent them from pursuing public office. These effects endure long after shifts in women's social and economic status by negatively influencing women's decisions to run as well as elites' evaluations of potential female candidates. These beliefs are compounded by the media, which frequently draw on gender stereotypes in ways that appear to negatively affect women's chances of getting elected. Nonetheless, in some countries arguments making reference to women's roles in the private sphere have served as powerful arguments for political inclusion. Furthermore, voter stereotypes may favor female candidates when feminine qualities are viewed as desirable at particular moments in time.

Gender and Routes to Political Office

Explanations of women's entry into positions of executive and legislative leadership thus focus on a combination of social, economic, cultural, and political reasons for women's inclusion and exclusion as political actors. . . .

Taking a closer look at the types of offices that women have held, it is striking to note that most female leaders—37, or 67 percent—are from dual executive systems, therefore sharing power with another executive. Women thus serve more often in systems where executive authority is more dispersed, as opposed to in those with more unified executive structures. Furthermore, in most of these cases, women tend to be placed in positions of weaker authority. Several of the female presidents elected by the public, for example, hold relatively nominal positions, serving mainly as figureheads. As such, Mary McAleese of Ireland has very little substantive power as compared to the prime minister. In other instances, female presidents bypass the public because they are elected by legislatures or replace male presidents from the position of vice-president. In addition to this, there are numerous examples of weak female prime ministers operating under much stronger presidents. This is typically the case for women in Africa, who are often unilaterally appointed by the president and frequently subject to dismissal at his will. The same is true of several female leaders in Eastern Europe. Consequently, not all national leadership posts are created equal. The fact that women have increased their numbers as executives is important. However, the specific powers and level of autonomy at their disposal are crucial in assessing how far they have come.

The lack of progress on several fronts . . . reveals that politics is still largely viewed as a "man's world."

Nevertheless, a substantial number of women have recently risen to important positions where their power is unchallenged by another executive. This is the case for several prime ministers in unified parliamentary systems, as well as for the few female presidents elected directly by the public in presidential systems. Interestingly, most of these women serve as presidents in Latin America and South and Southeast Asia, where women's education, economic, and political status lags behind that of men. In contrast to other regions, working their way up the party ranks is not the dominant path to power for women in these countries. These patterns can instead be explained in terms of familial ties. As previously noted, the reliance on marital or blood connections of women in politics in these parts of the world is not new. However, it has clearly not ceased. In fact, no woman holding dominant executive power in Latin America or Asia has ever come to power without familial connections. Moreover, popular election appears to be limited to women from political families. . . .

Despite Significant Gains, Gender Remains an Issue

Women have made dramatic gains in world politics in recent years. Although women still do not occupy half of all positions of executive and legislative leadership, a survey of global trends is encouraging: women appear to have shattered the political "glass ceiling" in countries with a diverse array of social, economic, cultural, and political characteristics. Further, these developments appear to have spilled over into other realms of political leadership. Most notably, there are now record numbers of women in cabinets, 16 percent overall. Two countries have surpassed the 50 percent mark, Finland and Norway, and 22 countries have more than 30 percent female ministers. In addition, 28 women now serve as speakers of parliament, about half of these in Latin America and the Caribbean. At the same time, there appear to be important role model effects when it comes to female presidents and prime ministers: 15 countries have had not just one female leader, but two different female leaders. This suggests that the presence of one woman in high political office may serve to break the strong association between masculinity and leadership. Obviously, this has not been the case in every country: for example, it has been nearly 20 years since Margaret Thatcher left office in the UK [United Kingdom]. However, combined with trends in many countries suggesting that patterns of recruitment to national parliaments are beginning to be re-gendered, these developments point to intriguing new possibilities with regard to women, gender, and politics.

The question remains, nonetheless, as to the broader meanings of these developments for women as a group. The lack of progress on several fronts, including the gendered conditions of women's access, the experiences and portrayals of female politicians, and the far from equal levels of executive and legislative representation, reveals that politics is still largely viewed as a "man's world." Further, the women who reach top political positions do not always seek to promote women as a group. Leaders like Gandhi, Meir, and Thatcher invoked masculine styles of leadership and did not take steps to improve women's status during their tenures in office. In contrast, others like Bachelet, Johnson-Sirleaf, and Gro Harlem Brundtland of Norway actively recruited women to cabinet positions and have advocated women-friendly public policies. Similarly, the women who achieve seats in parliament through gender quotas express varying degrees of commitment to women's issues. While some introduce a broad range of proposals aimed at helping women, others are constrained actively by the male leaders who appoint them or more indirectly by self-imposed concerns to avoid being marginalized in parliament by focusing only on a "narrow" set of issues related to women. These patterns indicate that gendered power dynamics are still very much at work in the political sphere, offering an important corrective to naïve optimism regarding the gains that women have made. Indeed, several months after their victories seemed assured, Benazir Bhutto had been assassinated and Hillary Clinton had dropped out of the presidential race. Women's progress in the political sphere is thus in flux, with few guarantees regarding their future success.

CHAPTER 3

Does the Participation of Women Improve Politics?

Overview: Most People Believe Men and Women Make Equally Good Leaders

Pew Research Center

The Pew Research Center is a nonpartisan organization that provides facts and data on the issues, attitudes, and trends shaping America and the world.

Americans believe women have the right stuff to be political leaders. When it comes to honesty, intelligence and a handful of other character traits they value highly in leaders, the public rates women superior to men, according to a new [August 25, 2008] nationwide Pew Research Center Social and Demographic Trends survey.

Nevertheless, a mere 6% of respondents in this survey of 2,250 adults say that, overall, women make better political leaders than men. About one-in-five (21%) say men make the better leaders, while the vast majority—69%—say men and women make equally good leaders.

The paradox embedded in these survey findings is part of a wider paradox in modern society on the subject of gender and leadership. In an era when women have made sweeping strides in educational attainment and workforce participation, relatively few have made the journey all the way to the highest levels of political or corporate leadership.

Why not? In the survey, the public cites gender discrimination, resistance to change, and a self-serving "old boys club" as reasons for the relative scarcity of women at the top. In somewhat smaller numbers, respondents also say that women's family responsibilities and their shortage of experience hold them back from the upper ranks of politics and business.

What the public does not say is that women inherently lack what it takes to be leaders. To the contrary, on seven of eight leadership traits measured in this survey, the public rates women either better than or equal to men.

Men and women tie on two of the next three traits on the public's ranking of leadership qualities measured in this survey—hard work and ambition.

For example, half of all adults say women are more honest than men, while just one-in-five say men are more honest (the rest say they don't know or volunteer the opinion that there's no difference between the sexes on this trait). And honesty, according to respondents, is the most important to leadership of any of the traits measured in the survey.

The next most important leadership trait, in the public's view, is intelligence. Here again, women outperform men: 38% of respondents say women are smarter than men, while just 14% say men are smarter, and the remainder say there's no difference between the sexes.

Men and women tie on two of the next three traits on the public's ranking of leadership qualities measured in this survey—hard work and ambition. Men prevail over women on decisiveness (their lone "victory" in the battery of eight traits), with 44% of respondents saying that men are more decisive and 33% saying women are.

Finally, women have big leads over men on the last three traits on the public's rankings of the eight items measured: being compassionate (80% say women; 5% say men); being outgoing (47% say women; 28% say men) and being creative (62% say women; 11% say men).

For anyone keeping score, that's women over men by five to one, with two ties, on eight traits, each of which at least two-thirds of the public says is very important or absolutely essential to leadership. Notably, nearly all of these gender evaluations are shared by men as well as women, though the margins are more heavily pro-woman among female respondents than among male respondents.

Women emerge from this survey a bit like a sports team that racks up better statistics but still loses the game.

The survey also asked respondents to assess whether men or women in public office are better at handling a range of policy matters and job performance challenges. On the policy front, women are widely judged to be better than men at dealing with social issues such as health care and education, while men have a big edge over women in the public's perception of the way they deal with crime, public safety, defense and national security.

As for job performance skills, women get higher marks than men in all of the measures tested: standing up for one's principles in the face of political pressure; being able to work out compromises; keeping government honest; and representing the interests of "people like you."

Overall, however, women emerge from this survey a bit like a sports team that racks up better statistics but still loses the game—witness the tiny 6% sliver of the public that says women generally make better political leaders than men.

To be sure, the fact that such a large majority of respondents (69%) say that women and men make equally good political leaders is itself a measure of the profound changes in women's role in society that have taken place over the past several decades.

Women make up 57% of all college students, about half of all law and medical school students, and more than four-in-ten students who earn masters degrees in business. They make up 46% of the total private sector workforce and 38% of all managers.

However, it's still lonely for women at the very highest rungs of the corporate and political ladder. Women are just 2% of the CEOs of the nation's Fortune 500 companies. In the political realm, they make up just 17% of all members of the U.S. House of Representatives; 16% of all U.S. senators; 16% of all governors; and 24% of all state legislators. Internationally, the U.S. ranks in the middle range—85th in the world—in its share of women in the lower house of its national legislative body.

Asked what accounts for this slow movement toward gender parity in top political positions, about half (51%) of all survey respondents say a major reason is that Americans simply aren't ready to elect a woman to high office; more than four-in-ten (43%) say a major reason is that women who are active in politics are held back by men, and 38% say a major reason is that women are discriminated against in all realms of society, and politics is no exception. These are the three most prevalent choices among seven possible explanations presented in the survey.

Next in the pecking order of explanations is the time pressure that comes with trying to balance work and family; 27% of the public cites this as a major reason there aren't more women leaders in politics. Some 26% say that a big reason is that women don't have the experience required for higher office. The least common explanations—chosen as a major reason by just 16% and 14% of respondents, respectively—are that women don't make as good leaders as men and that women aren't tough enough for politics.

Women Are Better Politicians than Men

Sarah Galer

Sarah Galer is a writer and media contact for the University of Chicago News Office.

Congresswomen consistently outperform their male counterparts on several measures of job performance, according to a recent study by University of Chicago scholar Christopher Berry.

The research comes as the 112th Congress is sworn in this month [January 2011] with 89 women, the first decline in female representation since 1978. The study authors argue that because women face difficult odds in reaching Congress—women account for fewer than one in six representatives—the ones who succeed are more capable on average than their male colleagues.

Study Findings

Women in Congress deliver more federal projects to their home districts than men do, even when controlling for such factors as party affiliation and ideology, according to the research by Berry, Assistant Professor in the Harris School of Public Policy Studies, and his former student Sarah Anzia, MPP [masters degree in public policy] '07, now a doctoral student at Stanford University. Congresswomen also sponsor and co-sponsor more legislation than their male counterparts, the authors found. The study has recently been accepted for publication at the *American Journal of Political Science*.

Sarah Galer, "Women in Congress Outperform Men on Some Measures, Harris School Study Finds," *University of Chicago News*, January 25, 2011. news.uchicago.edu. Reproduced by permission.

The authors interpret their findings as a by-product of voter discrimination against female candidates. When women confront such bias, only the most talented, politically ambitious females will attempt to run for office, and voters will tend to elect the most highly capable women. Because of one or both of these factors, the women elected will on average be higher performing than their male colleagues.

Congresswomen on average obtain 9 percent more in federal discretionary programs for their home districts—about $49 million per year—than congressmen.

"Women run for and are elected to public office at lower rates than men. This might be because women perceive themselves as less qualified to run than they actually are, or it might be because bias against women in the electorate produces a barrier to entry for them," Berry said. "In either case, the central implication of sex-based political selection is that the women we observe in office will, on average, outperform the men."

Measuring Performance

Since there is no direct way to measure legislator capability, the researchers measured performance in two ways. First, using Federal Assistance Award Data, a comprehensive compilation of federal domestic spending programs, the authors examined data from 1984 to 2004 showing the amount of federal program dollars that members of Congress brought to their home districts. The analysis encompassed discretionary spending, including most earmarks, but not entitlement programs or defense spending and other procurement programs.

Berry and Anzia found that congresswomen on average obtain 9 percent more in federal discretionary programs for their home districts—about $49 million per year—than congressmen, even when taking into account variables such as party affiliation, majority party status, seniority, electoral vulnerability, ideology, committee assignments, and district traits.

The authors also compared changes over time in spending within districts, to gauge how much a given district received when represented by a woman rather than a man. This method ensured that the estimated advantage for females was not simply a result of the types of districts they represent.

Second, the researchers examined the policymaking activities of women and men in Congress. They found that women sponsor and co-sponsor significantly more bills than men, and that bills sponsored by women get more co-sponsorship support from their colleagues. More generally, congresswomen score higher on various statistical measures of "network centrality," meaning that they have stronger networks of collaboration than their male counterparts.

"Two fundamental jobs of congressional representatives are constituency service, which includes bringing home federal projects as well as other direct work with constituents, and legislating, which means writing bills and shepherding them through the lawmaking process," said Berry. "The evidence shows that the women in Congress outperform the men on both levels."

When sex discrimination is present among voters, women must be better than their male counterparts to be elected.

The Jackie Robinson Effect

In what they dub "the Jackie (and Jill) Robinson Effect," Berry and Anzia relate this "sex-based selection" to the experience of Jackie Robinson, the first African American to play Major League Baseball. It is not surprising that Robinson is widely considered to be one of the best players in the sport's history, argue the authors, because he had to be the best in order to overcome the racial discrimination of the time.

Similarly, women running for Congress must be more motivated and more highly qualified than their male counterparts to win a seat. In fact, the worse the voter discrimination against women, the better women from those districts fare in Congress: the researchers found that congresswomen elected in more conservative districts, where they may face greater sex-based selection, achieve even larger advantages in spending than the average congresswomen.

"We emphasize that we are not arguing that women have more innate political talent than men, nor do we claim that all female candidates outperform their male counterparts," Berry said. He pointed out that widows who enter Congress to fill their deceased husbands' seats do not outperform congressmen, possibly because they bypassed the sex-based selection of elections.

"Our theory simply identifies a connection between the economics of discrimination and models of political agency: when sex discrimination is present among voters, women must be better than their male counterparts to be elected," Berry said.

Women Politicians Are Involved in Fewer Sex Scandals than Male Politicians

Lane Wallace

Lane Wallace is a writer, columnist, author, pilot, and entrepreneur who has written books for the National Aeronautics and Space Administration (NASA) and who won an award for the 2006 documentary, Breaking the Chain.

Nearly two years ago, when South Carolina Governor Mark Sanford admitted . . . to having an extra-marital affair with an Argentine woman, a lot of questions were raised about why this kind of scandal so rarely happens with women politicians. One answer offered was simply that there aren't that many women politicians in office.

It's true, of course. Women only make up 16.4% of the current [112th] Congress, and 12% of the nation's governors. But in a 2009 *Newsweek* tally of political sex scandals since 1976, only one out of 53 instances involved a woman politician (former Idaho Congresswoman Helen Chenoweth, who admitted to having an eight-year affair with a married rancher in the 1980s). So women aren't even holding up their fair percentage of the scandals.

Married people from all walks in life have extra-marital affairs. According to a 2006 report on American Sexual Behavior as part of the General Social Survey (GSS), an average of 16–18% of all married people have had an extra-marital affair. That's a considerably lower number than is often bandied about in the popular press, of course, which Tom Smith, the report's author, attributes to the lack of scientific rigor in the studies reporting higher numbers. He cites a number of studies that mirror the GSS results. But even in the GSS results, almost twice as many men had had extramarital affairs than women.

Explaining the Male-Female Gap

Why is that? Many reasons, to be sure. But the two scandals grabbing the headlines this week [May 19, 2011] (the arrest of IMF [International Monetary Fund] managing director Dominique Strauss-Kahn for sexual assault and the admission of former California Governor Arnold Schwarzenegger to fathering a child with a member of his household staff), point to a couple of factors that help explain that gap.

One has to do with what we typically consider attractive and/or sexy in men versus women. For better or worse . . . as a culture, we see competence and power as very attractive features in a man. The more power and competence a man and his position (and money) denote, the more attractive he will seem to a whole host of women. This, by the way, explains the appeal of the military flight suit. I single out the flight suit, as opposed to military dress uniforms, because there is nothing inherently attractive in what military pilots refer to as their "green bags." And yet, a pilot walking into a bar in one increases his chances of getting a date by an order of magnitude over a guy in a t-shirt and jeans. Why? Because the flight suit denotes competence and a certain level of power.

A woman pilot wearing a flight suit into a bar, on the other hand, will see her chances of a date fall. Why? Because (and again, this is a general trend, there are always exceptions), we don't see competence and power as sexy in a woman. If anything, they're threatening. When I bought my current airplane 12 years ago, (a simple, four-seat, single engine model), a male friend of mine congratulated me on the purchase, but then added,

"You know, Lane, this is not exactly going to help your love life."

Is that image changing? Of course it is. More and more men are waking up to the benefits and appeal of a smart, competent, independent and powerful woman. But as a culture, what makes a woman appealing is still her looks, not her power.

Sex as a Reward for Achieving Power

So how does this relate to political sex scandals? Well, one reason floated for the seemingly high number of politicians being caught cheating is that so much more opportunity may exist for them to stray. The theory goes that a politician (or star athlete, for that matter) will find a dizzyingly high number of adoring admirers at their disposal. And that theory may be true ... but I would argue that phenomenon is one known far better by male politicians than female ones. Why? Because the very features that make a male politician so much more attractive to people they meet (power and competence) make their female counterparts *less* sexually attractive, at least in many people's eyes.

Culturally, men are more likely to link power with a sense of entitlement about rewards that include sex.

But there's a second aspect of the power/sex connection that also helps explain the gap in sexual misconduct. And that's simply the sense of entitlement that some men have about sex, in terms of it being a kind of reward for achieving power, and a way of reassuring themselves about their hold on that power.

The link undoubtedly dates back to the days of conquering, raping and pillaging all being lumped together in the spoils of warrior combat. Win the battle, gain the power, and take the sex you want. That's not acceptable in today's more civilized society, of course, but a piece of it endures and surfaces more often than we'd like to admit. The atrocities in the Congo aside (where rape still IS a prevalent spoil of war), there's the bragging of [former professional basketball player] Magic Johnson about having had sex with a thousand women, the six-game suspension of [Pittsburgh] Steelers' quarterback Ben Roethlisberger for accusations of his assaulting and/or mistreating women, and even, on a much lesser scale, the dream many young men harbor of making it big on Wall Street so they can have a lot of women. I know women who have career aspirations on Wall Street, but none that involve making it big so they can have sex with a whole lot of men.

So even in consensual matters, there's a two-way dynamic with men in powerful positions that doesn't exist with women. Culturally, men are more likely to link power with a sense of entitlement about rewards that include sex, and there are many women who do, in fact, see a man as more sexually attractive if he's powerful. Hence you have Arnold Schwarzenegger having an affair with a member of his household staff, and President [Bill] Clinton having an affair with a young White House intern. If President Clinton had been a janitor instead of the President of the United States, [former White House intern] Monica Lewinsky would likely not have given him the time of day.

But that same link between power and sex lies behind sexual assault, as well. And that's where it really gets ugly. Any rape crisis counselor will tell you that rape (and sexual harassment, for that matter) is about power, not sex. Sex is just the tool—a way for an attacker to reassure himself of his power. An insecure man may use rape as a way to prove power he doesn't feel he has. But there's also the case of powerful men so used to getting their way with women that they can't imagine or handle any other outcome—which is one of the theories being floated to explain Strauss-Kahn's alleged behavior.

Women, Sex, and Power

The link between power and sex for women, on the other hand, has been to *withhold* it, not to force it. The plot of the Greek play *Lysistrata* even revolves around an agreement the women of Athens make with the women of Sparta to withhold sex from their husbands until both armies agree to stop fighting each other. So if anything, the power/sex link for women, if there is one, is a deterrent, not a catalyst. But most women in positions of power are also still far more concerned with being taken seriously than being seen as sexually attractive individuals. For men, the two go together. For women, the equation still involves opposite pulls—especially for women old enough to be in positions of political power.

Most women intuitively understand this dynamic, which is part of the reason why some of these politicians' behaviors make us so uncomfortable. If a man falls in love with someone other than his wife, it's certainly bad, and we thank our lucky stars that we're not the betrayed spouse in question, but it's easier to dismiss it as a private matter. But when we sense a power imbalance in the relationship, it makes it harder to compartmentalize a man's professional talents from his personal behavior. If we believe a man has crossed the line into sexual assault, most women would agree to cut him off at the knees (hence the drop in support for the Pittsburgh Steelers last fall among the team's female fans). But even if the behavior stays this side of legality, like affairs with household help or consenting but powerless young women, I think it gives us pause that extra-marital affairs between equals do not. Why? Because the abuse of that power is something that almost every woman, at one point or another, has had to deal with in the world. And we know just how awful, unjust and destructive a force it can be.

Sarah Palin's Self-Promotion Has Improved Politics for Other Women

Libby Copeland

Libby Copeland covers national politics for The Washington Post.

So Sarah Palin's not running [for president of the United States]. She broke the news on her own inimitable terms, not with a press conference but through a written statement and a radio appearance, near the end of the day's news cycle. "Not being a candidate, really, you're unshackled and you're allowed to be even more active," she told radio host Mark Levin. Still, despite her promises to remain unshackled and influential, this is surely the end of the Palin reign; without the possibility of a presidential run in her near future, she won't be commanding nearly as much media attention.

But even if you're one of the many who feel grateful at the prospect of hearing less from a certain woman from Wasilla [Alaska], it's worth considering what we might owe Palin. Politics aside (a big aside, but let's shelve them for the moment), Palin has excelled spectacularly at one thing that American women should feel grateful for: She is an exceedingly talented self-promoter. This is a big deal, because self-promotion is something that American women have historically been bad at, and they pay for that shortcoming in everything from mediocre salaries to thwarted ambitions.

A Good Thing for Women

Ever since the newly anointed vice-presidential candidate introduced herself to the nation three years ago by mocking

Barack Obama's lack of experience—"I guess a small-town mayor is sort of like a 'community organizer,' except that you have actual responsibilities"—a question has lingered in Sarah Palin's wake. Who does she think she is? Never mind that Palin's own lack of political experience was a liability for [former presidential candidate] John McCain. She has rarely underestimated her own potential. Last month [September 2011], the former Alaska governor corrected [conservative political commentator] Sean Hannity for leaving her off the list of most viable GOP [Republican] candidates, saying some polls showed her in the top three. She told another interviewer that although she could win the presidency, it might be too limiting. In her statement Wednesday [October 5, 2011], Palin suggested she could have just as much power without a "title," effectively arguing for herself as a kind of national organizer, albeit without actual responsibilities.

There will always be the unspoken rules that discourage female self-promotion, . . . in politics, which combines a conservative atmosphere with the job requirement of an inflated ego, the challenge for women is particularly acute.

Even when her logic is frustrating, even when she contradicts herself, Palin's unselfconscious brashness is a good thing for women because it is so needed and so exceptional. There are simply not enough women willing to tout their own greatness, to correct hosts who underestimate their popularity, to predict that, yes indeed, they could be elected president. This is in great part because women expect to be punished for anything that smacks of self-promotion. In *Necessary Dreams: Ambition in Women's Changing Lives*, psychiatrist Anna Fels compiles a disheartening litany of quotes from successful women undervaluing their own achievements. Prominent architect Laurinda Spear describes herself as a "totally bumbling person." [architect and sculptor] Maya Lin says she's lucky she's so small because it means people don't see her. Women interviewing for professorships at Harvard Law School routinely couch their responses in apologies.

"Conveying their strengths and attainments to others is so far from the expected female style of self-effacement that women experience it as 'bragging,'" Fels writes. She points out that females are denied recognition starting as early as preschool, when studies show that boys get more attention, more direction, and more "physical and verbal rewards." Science journalist Shankar Vedantam describes this extra credit given to men as the "invisible current" pushing boys toward the shore, persuading them that they are faster, stronger. Is it any wonder, then, that so many women internalize the notion that recognition does not rightly belong to them, that it is their destiny to listen and nod and admire? Is it any wonder that they don't ask for raises while their male counterparts do? A few years ago, Nicholas Kristof summed up the research on how people view ambitious women, pointing out that identical speeches are rated higher when they are believed to come from men: "A woman can be perceived as competent or as likable, but not both."

[Sarah Palin] has expanded the palette of permissible behavior for political women, hopefully for good.

There will always be the unspoken rules that discourage female self-promotion, particularly in the field of entertainment. But in politics, which combines a conservative atmosphere with the job requirement of an inflated ego, the challenge for women is particularly acute. Earlier this year, a University of Chicago political scientist found that female members of Congress sponsor more legislation and bring home more federal projects than do their male counterparts. Why? Christopher Berry speculated that only an elite group possessed of uncommon talent and ambition are able to push through the biases against women running for office.

And even those select women who do run are not immune to limiting expectations. Pat Schroeder has said her entry into politics started as a joke, until "we realized it wasn't so absurd." Barbara Boxer was described as arrogant last year by her female opponent, Carly Fiorina, for asking to be called "senator" instead of "ma'am." And it's no coincidence that [US Secretary of State] Hillary Clinton, whose ambition is routinely lampooned, has garnered the most sympathy during moments of vulnerability—those slight tears in New Hampshire during 2008; the marital humiliations care of Bill; the pushy tactics of her Senate race opponent, Rick Lazio, during a 2000 debate—not during moments of brazenness.

In the face of all this, Palin's public proclamations of self-confidence have been pretty remarkable. "You know, I do go rogue and I call it like I see it," she told [politican commentator] Greta Van Susteren last month. "I don't mind stirring it up in order to get people to think and debate aggressively, and to find solutions to the problems that our country is facing." Whether or not she has the goods to back any of this up is in some sense beyond the point. Palin may not realize it, but her real legacy lies elsewhere: She has expanded the palette of permissible behavior for political women, hopefully for good.

More Female Politicians May Not Mean Better Results

Kay Hymowitz

Kay Hymowitz is an author and writer, the William E. Simon Fellow at the Manhattan Institute, a public policy think tank, and a contributing editor at the Institute's City Journal. *She writes about gender issues, families, marriage, poverty, and inequality.*

Kirsten Gillibrand, the likeable junior senator from my home state of New York, has been promoting a new initiative this past week. It's called OfftheSidelines and its purpose is to get more women into the political fray. . . . It sounds like one of those efforts to which no sensible person could possibly object. But that's not the reason I'm having qualms about it.

No, the reason is this: Gillibrand is operating under assumptions about what women want that don't hold up to close scrutiny. I have written about this at greater length elsewhere, but let me sum up this way. Like many liberal-leaning women, Gillibrand assumes that bringing more of the fair sex into politics means more attention for what are commonly called "women's issues." These are issues like child care, discrimination, abortion, parental leave, and the like. Here's Gillibrand speaking at a recent dinner: "They [Congressional Republicans] also, while they were at it, defunded early childhood education, nutrition for women and infants. Everything that women care about in this country has been placed on the chopping block. Everything." Notice the unspoken premise: Women care about nutrition and preschool as *political* issues. That is, they believe government should take the lead.

Republican Women's Issues

But the 2010 election has upended this assumption. Women like [2008 Republican vice presidential candidate] Sarah Palin, [Congresswoman from Minnesota] Michele Bachmann, and the many other XX conservatives who gained traction during the mid term election weren't talking about child care, equal pay initiatives, or any other issue in the familiar agenda. Instead, they were talking about government debt and patronage, about bailouts and excessive regulation. And they often did so in explicitly female terms: "I think a whole lot of moms . . . are concerned about government handing our kids the bill;" Palin once said. "We're stealing opportunities from the future of America."

By all means, let's encourage more women to go into politics. But don't count on celebrating the results.

In the Mamma Grizzly brand of politics, a trillion dollar deficit *is* a woman's issue. And so is what they view as excessive government spending. In keeping with fears about ballooning deficits as well as their frontiersy individualism, conservative women voters are skeptical of judicial "overreach" and government bureaucracies (though Palin has credited Title IX[1] for her success on the basketball court and for encouraging her competitive spirit). Anti-discrimination legislation, day care inititiatives, whatever; they cost too much and they're not what government should be doing anyway. This is the very opposite of what Gillibrand has in mind when she calls for more women to get off the sidelines.

To be sure, neither Palin nor Bachmann nor any other Grizzly represents the majority of the fair sex. But that's my point: neither does Gillibrand or her organization. The 2010

---

1. Title IX is a US law enacted in 1972 barring discrimination on the basis of sex from participation in education programs receiving federal funding.

election should have made that clear. Red state women substantially increased their numbers in Congress and in state legislatures where future Congresswomen, Senators and Governors are on deck. The seemingly permanent gender gap that had women reliably voting Democratic started to erode. For the first time since 1982 when exit polls began looking at Congressional races, Republicans received a majority of women's votes.

By all means, let's encourage more women to go into politics. But don't count on celebrating the results.

.

Women Cannot Rule the World Like Men

Sandra Tsing Loh

Sandra Tsing Loh is a writer, commentator, author of several books, and a contributing editor for The Atlantic. *She also is a musician and theater performer who has appeared in a number of solo off-Broadway shows.*

I have accorded former White House press secretary Dee Dee Myers the apparently unusual honor of actually reading her book, *Why Women Should Rule the World*, and I will now discuss it, whether you want me to or not. . . .

Women as Consensus-Builders

Myers begins by stroking the feminine ego, if in a somewhat bland, business-book way: women *should* rule the world, the flap copy of her book asserts, simply because "women tend to be better communicators, better listeners, better at forming consensus." Too, women are more practical than men. . . . Smart and tough, females have proved their excellence in the traditionally male fields—politics, business, science, and academia—that Myers suggests define public life, and she illustrates her points with a triumphal roll call of successful female CEOs [chief executive officers], hard-driving female senators and governors, [primatologist and chimpanzee expert] Jane Goodall, and a Third World Nobel Peace Prize winner with whose work I was not familiar but with whom clearly any sensible person would be hard-pressed to find fault. In short, as the jacket avers somewhat anodynely,

In a highly competitive and increasingly fractious world, women possess the kind of critical problem-solving skills that are urgently needed to break down barriers, build understanding, and create the best conditions for peace.

With more women in power, the world would be better off. Specifically? "Politics would be more collegial. Businesses would be more productive. And communities would be healthier."

And yet, Myers maintains, for all our superior communicating, listening, and consensus building, the percentage of women at the highest levels of even the reasonably enlightened U.S. government is still woefully small, about 15 percent. Why *don't* women rule the world? Because even bright women aren't always allowed to shine in the Company of Men.

In support, she presents her own story. On the one hand, she still considers it an honor to have been chosen, in 1993, as the first female—and, at 31, one of the youngest ever—White House press secretary. She understands that, thanks to Bill Clinton's pledge to have a staff that "looked like America," she actually benefited by being a woman. On the other hand, Myers says she suffered the peculiarly female fate of having "responsibility without corresponding authority." She was expected to hold at bay the press wolves of the briefing room without having access to the most up-to-date information shared by Clinton's true inner circle, largely—it is fair to say—a boys' club.

In Myers's formulation, women leaders are grown-up Girl Scouts who work toward their noble, humanistic . . . goals cheerfully and with just a little bit of moxie.

Her authority was further diminished by having to share her position, in a highly unorthodox arrangement. Although Myers was awarded the title of press secretary, the new "director of communications," George Stephanopoulos, would assume the press secretary's customary daily briefings (Myers would be "backup" briefer), the higher rank of "assistant to the president" (Myers would be "deputy assistant"), the press secretary's traditional spacious West Wing office (Myers was assigned a smaller one), and, of course, the higher salary. Overall, it seems that Myers—who admits to struggling before the camera to get even her outfits and hair right—was outfoxed by George in every way. . . .

If we want women to compete as rulers, . . . *shouldn't we be able to do everything men do, succeeding if need be as competitive, manipulative, backstabbing, foulmouthed egomaniacs?*

So as far as women ruling in politics, the tally would appear to be: Women are smart, principled, professional, cordial—and just a bit dull. . . . Men are conniving, crude, backbiting—and lively. In Myers's formulation, women leaders are grown-up Girl Scouts who work toward their noble, humanistic (and at the same time, deftly bottom-line-enhancing) goals cheerfully and with just a little bit of moxie. The role models Myers celebrates include not [US Secretary of State] Hillary Clinton nor [former US Secretary of State] Condoleezza Rice . . . but the country's 16 genial female senators, who even in today's climate have reached across the aisle, forged friendships, and cooperated on issues. . . .

At this point, I added *The Architect: Karl Rove and the Dream of Absolute Power* to my growing, unhappy heap of political biographies. . . . My gloom deepened as I read about Rove's [senior advisor to former president George W. Bush] vast, conspiratorial, conservative stealth fog, a fog microdirected by Rove not during official meetings in the White House but during rendezvous on rainy Washington side streets. . . . So while Myers's estimable high-mindedness about women is understandable for a person who cites, as youthful inspiration, [former astronaut] Sally Ride . . . , if we want women to compete as *rulers*, I began to think, shouldn't we be able to do everything men do, succeeding if need be as competitive, manipulative, backstabbing, foulmouthed egomaniacs? Consider dragon ladies Leona Helmsley (ran her own hotel chain), Judith Regan (ran her own O.J. [Simpson]-friendly publishing imprint), and *Vogue's* Anna "Nuclear" Wintour, so legendary in her frosty evil. Ah, the state of the world! Here is the one . . . female who could prove to be a match for a sadistic Republican Master Planner. . . . But sadly, better lights like Dee Dee Myers have chosen safer, saner career paths—such as stay-at-home pundit.

When it comes to competition, . . . there goes the female advantage.

Not that (more bad news!) women are generally predisposed to zero-sum games like elections, anyway—the caribou-hunting Republican vice-presidential candidate [referring to Sarah Palin] notwithstanding. To my come-hither bedside stack, I added *The Sexual Paradox: Men, Women, and the Real Gender Gap,* by the Canadian psychologist Susan Pinker. Using the latest neurological and biological findings of brain-imaging and sex-hormone assays, Pinker adds scientific ballast to the anecdotal truisms that women are more consensus-minded and team-oriented, and are better at reading human visual cues, interpreting feelings, and maintaining relationships and relationship networks than men. Since you asked, females score high in math, too, but interestingly, unlike males, mathematically gifted females also tend to be high scorers in other areas, giving them more academic freedom to opt out.

Women and Competition

But when it comes to competition, in that great neuroendocrine smackdown, there goes the female advantage. Consider this startling study done with fourth-grade Israeli schoolchildren: when boys and girls each ran alone on a track, there was no measurable speed difference by gender. But when each child was teamed with another child and asked to run again, the boys ran faster and the girls ran slower—slowest of all when running against other girls! What females love is bonding, helping, sharing, and oxytocin—that "opiatelike hormone" dubbed by one anthropologist "the elixir of contentment." Forget all this tedious racing: what girls would really like to do is carry each other around the track—taking turns! Indeed, studies show that whereas competitive situations drive adrenaline increases in men, they drive adrenaline decreases in most women. Men associate more pleasurable feelings with competition than do women, and even "an eagerness to punish and seek revenge feels more fun." . . . Even more harrowing: for men, not only does the urge to punish correlate with an increase in testosterone, but testosterone can measurably spike when they touch a gun.

And that's just the dog-eat-dog male aggression you can see. Yet more pernicious is the result when that worldview is encoded, unquestioned, systemic. Indeed, the next layer of female radicalism belongs to those who argue that even the perception of money as a "measuring rod" is itself male-centric. In a hard-to-find yet truly groundbreaking book, *Counting for Nothing* (1988), Marilyn Waring, a lesbian goat farmer and member (then the youngest) of the New Zealand parliament, reveals few concerns about her hair and outfits and goes way beyond the trepidations and personal politics of being a female in a male-dominated government to hit back at—yes, and why not?—men, with a force so bracingly Old School as to be almost medieval. To one who came of age in the 1970s and '80s, when feminists had flowing hair and gypsy skirts, Waring's crew-cutted, steel-belted work is a shock. Formidably literate . . . and unflinchingly numerical . . . , Waring eschews metaphysical questions of female selfhood and uses *her* . . .

power to dive into a painstaking analysis of the United Nations System of National Accounts. . . .

As Waring hammers home with example after absurd example, policies that spring from building national GDPs [gross domestic product, a measure of a country's total economic output] can be destructive to the planet as well as to humans. In calculations of a GDP, a chemical spill is a good thing. . . . A beautiful mountain is worth zip, but strip-mining—now there you have your growth again. Fresh fruit picked off your tree—nada. If you want to create growth, you must buy packaged corn chips. "Peace" itself has no value in a war-based economy—so the value of "safety" is determined by the price people pay for it. . . .

Although Waring was not privy, in 1988, to the 21st-century neurobiological discoveries that Susan Pinker describes, she relentlessly ascribes certain behavioral traits to males. The free-market founder himself, 18th-century philosopher Adam Smith, "established the logical foundation for his work by identifying what he thought was essential human nature," she writes. "He developed an image of humans as materialistic, egoistic, selfish and primarily motivated by pursuit of their own self-interest." Quoting Smith:

> Man [sic] has almost constant occasion for the help of his brethren and it is in vain for him to expect it from their benevolence only . . . It is not from the benevolence of the butcher, the brewer, or the baker that we expect our dinner, but from their regard to their own interest.

As we now know, Smith's assertion would indeed be true in a world made up only of men. . . .

But fortunately, ours is not a world only of men.

Women's Power

All right, so what if wo-men are power-wielding-impaired? Is ruling the world the only way to change the world? Recently, prompted by yet another round of proposed California public-education budget cuts. . . . I decided, in the heat of motherly perimenopausal ire, to throw a grassroots protest on the front steps of the Sacramento Capitol. At 46—a bit too long in the tooth to be Gen X, while still having managed to miss Wood-stock—this was my very first street rally, so the skills I used (permit writing, release filing, Excel spreadsheeting) were those I'd acquired working for the PTA [parent teacher association] at my daughters' school. And while parents of both sexes seemed equally outraged about the budget cuts—many fathers passionately blogged about it and rapped out irate e-mails of "big ideas" . . . —it was only the mothers who rallied themselves, in groups of two, 10, and 30. It was . . . the mothers who packed 15-person vans with pillows and blankets at 2 a.m., cut up apples and oranges, and hammered stakes in our tent city of 100-plus people. . . .

While at a biological disadvantage in competitions, women . . . are at a clear advantage when it comes to grouping together and the activities that accompany it.

True, our little rally was nothing compared with Donna Dees-Thomases's Million Mom March on Washington in 2000, an event she chronicles in her astonishing . . . book, *Looking for a Few Good Moms*—a volume that contains the most dauntingly titled appendix I've ever seen: "How to Organize a Bus." Dees-Thomases quotes a man, Million Mom Marcher Bill Jenkins—whose 16-year-old son had been shot dead while working at a fast-food restaurant—on the political power of numbers in the crusade she and her grassroots horde are waging:

> There are two ways to hunt. In one, the hunter . . . enters the forest alone . . . This is how the gun industry has been fought in the past. Dedicated lawyers and lobbyists who

have learned its every move have been fighting one-on-one. Sometimes they have gotten clear shots and scored minor victories.

But there is another way to hunt ... The entire village enters the forest. Not highly trained, just willing participants. They beat the brush, driving the quarry to open ground, and surround it, and the hunt is over.

Given the apparent female ... aversion to competitive, winner-take-all activities like elections, ... democracy ... is clearly stacked against female candidates.

Crowding, in fact, may be more effective for women than ruling when it comes to changing the world. While at a biological disadvantage in competitions, women—who even make trips to restaurant bathrooms in pairs—are at a clear advantage when it comes to grouping together and the activities that accompany it: gossiping, sharing, bonding, assisting, scrapbooking, and building networks.

Given the apparent female neuroendocrinic aversion to competitive, winner-take-all activities like elections, unless testosterone shots become a new female norm, even democracy ..., with its boastful, chest-beating campaigning, is clearly stacked against female candidates. . . .

Barring such fantasies, we should learn to better organize our crowding. Today, the Barnes & Noble "Women's Studies" shelves are thick with books on women's self-esteem, on women's bodies, on women and money. But to exert more true power in the world, we need to pay less attention to our feelings. . . . Why in five decades of modern feminist writing have we never seen any serious consideration of, for instance, the PTA, a hugely powerful, 100-plus-year-old, women-founded and women-dominated organization, whose well-funded and effective lobbying arm can actually help push through legislation? The women's movement has ignored millions of PTA women—women busy baking brownies and zooming about in their Kohl's [department store] wear, who can't *rule* the world but who can *change* it. My fellow PTA mothers—"change agents" all—we need more books that teach us to build and direct our networks to do the work *we* value.

CHAPTER 4

What Steps Should Be Taken to Encourage More Women to Enter Politics?

Chapter Preface

Although women's participation in politics has increased in recent decades, both in the United States and in countries around the world, most commentators agree that women are still underrepresented in the majority of national legislatures. The global average number of legislative or parliamentary seats held by women is a mere 18.4 percent, even though women typically make up about 50 percent of national populations. Various strategies have been proposed to increase women's representation in politics, and some countries have implemented electoral system changes that have produced remarkable improvements in the number of women in elected legislation positions.

One such system, gender quotas, requires that women be represented in political bodies according to a set number or percentage. There are different kinds of quotas, some legally binding and mandatory (based on a constitutional provision or law), and others voluntarily agreed to in order to increase numbers of women in politics. Quotas also can take the form of reserved legislative seats, setting aside positions specifically for women; party quotas, adopted by political parties; or legislative quotas, requiring that all parties nominate a certain proportion of women. Quotas thus can be used either in the nominating process, to make sure that women at least get on the ballot, or they can be results-oriented, setting aside a mandatory number of seats for women at the end of the election process.

More than one hundred countries around the globe, both developed and less developed, have implemented some form of gender quota systems, and most of these have appeared in the past fifteen years. In the developed world, for example, France changed its constitution in 1999 to state that women and men should have equal access in electoral and elective matters. A year later, French law was rewritten to require that political parties nominate equal numbers of men and women for most elections, including the presidency. Another European nation, Spain, set a 40 percent quota for women parliamentary candidates in 2007. Belgium and Slovenia also set mandatory quotas (both requiring 33 percent female representation on national electoral lists). Similarly, Argentina adopted a 30 percent quota for women on electoral lists. Finland, meanwhile, requires that various decisionmaking bodies have at least 40 percent representation by women. Several other Scandinavian countries—including Sweden, Iceland, the Netherlands, and Norway—have voluntary political party quotas for women.

In the developing world, India's law imposes a 33 percent quota on each of its three levels of local government. Other developing countries with mandatory quotas (sometimes called reserves) include Pakistan (which requires that 17.5 percent of the National Assembly seats be held by women), Nepal (where women must constitute 50 percent of any party's candidates), Bangladesh (which reserves forty-five out of 345 legislative seats for women), and Rwanda (which reserves thirty out of 100 legislative seats for women). South Africa, meanwhile, adopted a voluntary 30 percent quota for women in its National Congress.

Countries that have embraced gender quotas rank high in terms of female political representation. According to 2011 United Nations data,[1] for example, Rwanda is the only nation in the world with more women than men (56.3 percent) in its national legislature. Rwanda therefore tops the global list of nations with high female representation, followed by other countries with quota systems—for example, Sweden (45 percent), South Africa (44.5 percent), Iceland (42.9 percent), the Netherlands (40.7 percent), Norway (39.6 percent), and Argentina (38.5 percent). In fact, of the top twenty countries with the highest proportion of women in their national legislatures, seventeen have some form of a quota system.

Also, many countries that were once very low on this list have seen remarkable improvements in the percentage of legislative seats held by women by using quotas. Rwanda, for example, ranked 24th in 1995, but jumped to first following the introduction of quotas. Similarly, South Africa, ranked 141st in the percentage of legislative seats held by women in the 1990s, but now is ranked third (44.5 percent). Finland's quota law, too, resulted in an increase in women's political participation from 25 percent in 1980 to 40 percent today. And Argentina, which now boasts 38.5 percent female representation in its legislature, also elected a woman, Cristina Fernández de Kirchner, as president in 2007. A number of other examples of quota successes can be cited as well—for example, Pakistan (22.2 percent of national legislative seats held by women), Nepal (33.2 percent), and Bangladesh (18.6 percent).

In many cases, quota systems were adopted as a result of proposals from women's groups. Quota supporters often argue that they not only increase diversity in government, but also elevate the level of attention paid to women's issues and help to legitimize the role of female politicians in public attitudes. Critics have complained, however, that quotas sometimes bring unqualified women into legislatures, thereby reinforcing stereotypes about women's inability to compete in politics. Many people think that gender quotas are unlikely to be considered in the United States due to negative public attitudes about quotas as a tool for social engineering. The authors of the viewpoints in this chapter suggest a number of other ways to encourage women to become involved in US and world politics.

Notes

1. "Millenium Development Goals Indicators: Seats Held by Women in National Parliament, Percentage," United Na-

tions Statistics Division, Department of Economic and Social Affairs, United Nations, August 2011. http://unstats .un.org/unsd/mdg/SeriesDetail.aspx?srid=557.

Removing Barriers to Women in Politics Is Not Enough

Joelle Schmitz

Joelle Schmitz is a Fulbright scholar and a senior fellow at the Harvard University Mossavar-Rahmani Center for Business and Government.

Headlines would have us believe that we're witnessing a government takeover by snarling "Mama Grizzlies." But, within its coverage of the new political animal, the news media miss the forest for the trees. A truer danger lies in the obfuscation of harsher realities that are not as well represented by [2008 Republican vice presidential candidate] Sarah Palin and [governor of South Carolina] Nikki Haley as they are by the numbers 89 and 2012.

Eighty-nine is the number of nations that still surpass the U.S. in terms of women's representation in government. Some nations not known for human rights. Nations such as Rwanda, Uganda, Tajikistan, South Africa and Cuba. Given all its wealth and principle, our country still ranks an embarrassing 90th out of 186 worldwide.

Clear Disadvantages

For decades within the U.S., female participation in political and business leadership has consistently stagnated around 18%. And, despite the "Grizzly" hype, no one is anticipating any real improvement this November [2010]. In fact, the total number of female congressional representatives could well decline for the first time in three decades.

The underrepresentation sparks the perennial question: Why?

Joelle Schmitz, "Women in Politics? The U.S. Is Failing," *USA Today*, October 12, 2011. usatoday.com. Reproduced by permission.

Most pundits suggest "self-selection." In other words, that women are too busy upholding both careers and the majority of household responsibilities, they are half as likely to think they can win an election and less likely to feel they can amass the average $3 million necessary to secure a seat in Congress.

Statistics offer a more fundamental explanation:

- Men make up 83% of Congress.

- Incumbents win more than 90% of the time.

So despite the fact that women are just as likely to win open seats as men and just as likely to be able to draw the financial means, they remain at a structural disadvantage from which they are unlikely to achieve equality within our lifetimes.

Mandates for Female Representation

Indeed, the evolution of equality is rarely organic. Of the 25 nations that have realized a greater than 30% female participation in their governments, 90% required some form of temporary jump-start to secure permanent gains.

In March [2010], India voted to require 30% female representation in government. In January, France voted to require 40% female board membership in business. Today, half of all national governments include some form of legally required minimums for women, while the U.S. remains on the sidelines of an international race to equality. Our absence offers a clear reminder that other countries—and many countries considered less advanced—deal more openly than Americans on issues of gender inequity.

Though our own government would never consider such mandates, we could surely tackle the structural impediments to equal representation. The gender representation gap— women make up only 17% of Congress, but 51% of the U.S. population—demands as much.

The same could be argued for business, where subconscious hiring preferences yield their own "incumbency" biases.

In 2012, we have an opportunity to improve. That year, congressional districts will be redrawn on the basis of the 2010 Census, thereby creating new political territory devoid of the incumbency bias that perpetuates gender inequities.

It is not simply enough to remove barriers to participation in a country where women unaided have constituted only 2% of our government since 1789.

Indeed, denial of this problem is socially ingrained. Promising young women are encouraged to never mention gender inequities, but rather be good citizens and simply achieve without any reference to barriers even as they compromise that mandated achievement. Within upwardly mobile circles, the topic remains as taboo as mental health once was, and its avoidance as debilitating.

Still, as even [Chinese Communist leader] Mao Zedong recognized: women hold up "half the sky." Studies have shown that national competitiveness increases with gender parity. Countries deploying more resources produce more and influence more. We are thus encouraged to realize our shared values of equality and opportunity in order to strengthen our economy, better legitimize our government, and best position ourselves internationally.

What Can Be Done

While 2012 lends us the occasion to improve, even this opportunity will not sufficiently secure what the 1995 Beijing Conference on Women described as "equality of result." It is not simply enough to remove barriers to participation in a country where women unaided have constituted only 2% of our government since 1789.

Only abiding efforts may coalesce a critical mass toward "critical minority." Accordingly, since chief of staff positions supply our candidate pools, we could encourage our congressional members to hire female chiefs of staff in greater numbers than the current 33%. Since candidates, on average, must be asked several times to run, we could each encourage a woman via non-partisan programs such as sheshouldrun.org and runningstartonline.org.

Since gender-oriented comments disproportionately disadvantage women, we could promote gender-neutral political environments via initiatives such as the recently deployed Name It Change It.

And since the challenges facing female candidates remain unique, we could support non-profit, non-partisan organizations such as the White House Project, which remains committed against—and cognizant of—the disadvantages of disparity.

But until we develop some national clarity on the sobering realities behind the headlines, we will remain not only politically and economically underserved, but denied our greater American potential.

Recruitment and Training Can Bring More Young Women into Politics

Barbara Lee

Barbara Lee is president of the Barbara Lee Political Office and Barbara Lee Family Foundation, groups that seek to advance women's equality and representation in American politics and contemporary art.

Somewhere among the estimated 1.7 million new college graduates of the class of 2011 is the future of American politics. By the numbers, this should also mean a surge of new women leaders on the horizon. But even though 57 percent of students enrolled in college are women—a statistic that has held for more than a decade—the gender gap does not favor women once they leave campus.

Once women enter the job market or public office they're no longer in the lead. While women make up 67 percent of the American workforce, they earn 17 percent less than their male counterparts. Women comprise only 16 percent of Congress. For women to achieve equal pay at work and equal representation in government, we must invest in young women after they leave the classroom.

Education, Training, and Funding

The barriers to women entering politics are well-known and are not insurmountable: women need to be recruited, learn how to attract party support and raise funds, as well as overcome the increased scrutiny on how they will balance work and family. The Center for American Women in Politics at

Barbara Lee, "Pomp and Circumstance: Young Women and the Future of Politics," *The Huffington Post*, June 2, 2011. Huffingtonpost.com. Copyright © 2011 Barbara Lee. Reproduced by permission of the author.

Rutgers, in partnership with my foundation [Barbara Lee Family Foundation] studied women elected officials at the state level and concludes in their Poised to Run report that while women are underrepresented in state legislatures, the pool of women candidates is larger than commonly believed and more funding and training can help women win.

Engaging women while they are still in college is another key element in building the pipeline for women in politics.

Several partisan and non-partisan programs throughout the country are working to funnel that pool of talent into the pipeline of future women political leaders. By providing critical education, training, inspiration, and funding, these programs are bringing more young women in the political process.

Focusing on early recruitment and training, Running Start encourages girls to channel their interest into politics by selecting 50 school-aged girls from across the country to participate in their week-long Young Women's Political Leadership Training Program (YWPL) in Washington, D.C. each year. This year's [2011] graduates included 17-year-old Maria Peeples, a student activist from Wisconsin, who encouraged her state legislature to pass a comprehensive sex education bill and was on hand when the Governor signed it into law. Maria honed her skills in the program and was named a "Woman to Watch" at the Running Start awards gala earlier in May. Running Start also recently launched Elect Her, a program designed to encourage women to run for student government on campus since research has shown that women who run for student body elections in college are more likely to run for office as adults.

Engaging women while they are still in college is another key element in building the pipeline for women in politics.

Recent graduate Varina Winder said that in the Barbara Lee Women in US Politics Training Program at Harvard's Kennedy School of Government she learned from women experts and was inspired and supported by a network of women class-mates. "I view politics as a way to affect change on the issues about which I care," said Winder. "I think it's important that young women: 1) Vote!; 2) Know we can engage at any level and; 3) Realize that having young voices in politics brings a different perspective and added diversity."

Too often, women do not see themselves running for office so a pool of highly qualified Democratic candidates is being left untapped.

One of my Foundations's largest ongoing projects helps add more of those young voices to politics in Massachusetts. Our endowment to Simmons College—my alma mater—provides funding for an intern fellowship program at the Massachusetts State House. The program seeks to increase the number of young women who enter the pipeline of political leadership with exposure to and education in the nuts and bolts of Massachusetts politics. Over 80 young women have benefited from this mentor-based internship since it began in 2004.

Emerge Massachusetts is trying to bridge the political gen-der gap in my home state by training qualified women who may lack confidence that they are experienced enough to run for public office or who just don't know where to start. Emerge is the only in-depth, six-month training program that gives Democratic women in Massachusetts the tools they need to run and win. Judy Neufeld, Executive Director of Emerge MA and an alumna of the program herself, says that Emerge teaches women of diverse backgrounds how to think like a candidate. "I had run several campaigns before taking the pro-gram," Judy said, "and I thought I knew everything there was to know about campaigning, but I was so wrong! Emerge gave me the skills I would need as a candidate. Too often, women do not see themselves running for office so a pool of highly qualified Democratic candidates is being left untapped."

These are just a few of the programs throughout the country that are recruiting, training, and inspiring the next generation of women leaders. . . .

And if you are a recent graduate yourself, Congratulations! Have you considered running for office?

Women's Underrepresentation in Politics Should Not Be Blamed on a Lack of Political Ambition

J. Goodrich

J. Goodrich is an economist, writer, and blogger who has published articles in magazines, various political websites, and on Echidne of the Snakes, a blog site.

Imagine this: You are running for Congress, campaigning and trying to carry out all your usual obligations. Then one morning your home burns down. While you and your family escape unharmed, almost every single thing you owned has disappeared. How long would you take before you'd start campaigning again? Six months? A year? Never?

These events are not imaginary, but something which happened to Darcy Burner and her family [in Washington state] on the first of July [2008]. She took a campaign break of eighteen days. Eighteen days. Now that is some determination! We might even call this political ambition, a great desire to serve the public no matter what.

Burner is not the only woman who has demonstrated such stamina and focus in political life. Madeline Albright, the first female Secretary of State of the United States, once said that she wanted to do more than to just maintain the achievements of earlier Secretaries of State: she wanted to aim higher. Carol Moseley Brown had enough political ambition not only to become the first female African-American Senator in the United States Congress, but to run for the president of the

United States. And we are all familiar with [US Secretary of State] Hillary Clinton's recent presidential run and political ambition.

There is a substantial gender gap in political ambition; men tend to have it and women don't.

Inner Glass Ceilings?

Yet Ruth Marcus, a *Washington Post* columnist, thinks that it is the lack of political ambition which keeps women away from participating in political life. It's not discrimination that keeps the number of American women in Congress at 16 percent; the problem, she writes, is that women have an "inner glass ceiling": a tendency to give up too soon and too easily, a tendency to shirk away from the feistiness of political battles, a tendency to underrate their own abilities.

Marcus learned this from a recent [2008] Brookings Institution study by Jennifer L. Lawless and Richard L. Fox, which is summarized like this: "In this report, we argue that the fundamental reason for women's under-representation is that they don't run for office. There is a substantial gender gap in political ambition; men tend to have it and women don't."

It's certainly a convenient conclusion—If the reason for so few women in political decision-making roles is their own unwillingness to play the game, we as a society don't have to do anything to change the situation. It's up to women themselves to become more ambitious, and if they don't, well, perhaps it's all to do with biological differences between men and women. Right?

Caryl Rivers, a media critic, author and expert on the popularizations of gender science points out the great appeal of such explanations, especially now that the decoding of the human genome is in the news almost daily: "If you take the extreme view of gender differences as all biological, then if girls trail boys in math scores, say, no action is necessary. This despite the fact that Korean girls score higher than American boys."

Never mind if scientific studies show that things like the genetics of "political ambition" remain science-fiction; to appeal to biology allows us all not to worry about the effects of culture or gender roles in the division of labor. If glass ceilings are internal, then the problems belong to the individual women and individual women alone. Perhaps they are not problems at all, but Just The Way Things Are?

Obstacles for Women

I almost hesitate to break the peace and comfort of that explanation, but break it I must, if not for any other reason than the one that the Lawless and Fox study isn't about "political ambition" in the colloquial sense of the term . . . but about studying the process, which leads a qualified individual to either decide to run for political office or not.

For this purpose, the study selected several thousand men and women from the fields that are usually seen as good launching pads for political careers—law, business, education and political activism—and then asked them questions about their political plans, attitudes and life situations, both in 2001 and in 2008.

The most common reason women give when deciding not to run for office is, "maybe when the children are all grown." This has nothing to do with "political ambition."

The answers to these questions showed that equally qualified men and women may have different family responsibilities, different levels of external encouragement and support, different views about the political environment, different assessments about their own competence and different feelings about the negative aspects of campaigning. Some of these may be related to the way we usually understand the term "political ambition," but others have more to do with the institutional constraints of American politics or with socially accepted gender roles.

To give just one example of the latter, 60 percent of women with children in the study told the researchers that they were the primary caregivers for their children, while 60 percent of the men with children in the study described their partner as the primary caregiver. Given that all the study subjects already had careers, entering politics would mean a third job for these women but only a second job for the men.

The study design doesn't let us measure what the actual impact of the different family obligations might be, but Ilana Goldberg, whose organization She Should Run encourages women to run for elected office, says that the most common reason women give when deciding not to run for office is, "maybe when the children are all grown." This has nothing to do with "political ambition"—rather, it has everything to do with cultural expectations about who is responsible for the children and who has a built-in support system.

Cultural expectations also influence the amount of encouragement that men and women receive in pursuing their political goals. According to the study results, men were more likely than women to have been encouraged to run both by people in politics and by their friends and families (though this difference was reduced in the most recent round of the study by the efforts of advocacy groups who contact and encourage qualified women to seek office). Still, as Sandeep Kaushik of Darcy Burner's campaign noted, it is not unusual for women who run and lose their first race to be told that they "have had their turn" and that they should relinquish further thoughts of running, to step aside and to let someone else have a chance. Such values are embedded in the culture, not in the woman's own political ambition. But their final impact might well be to make women less likely to stay in politics.

Women's Political Participation in Other Countries

Let's add another layer of complication to the notion of an "internal glass ceiling" by noting that the United States ranks 68th in the world in the proportion of women in national legislatures. Either 67 countries have women with more ambitious genes or both cultural values and the institutional aspects of political systems matter. It also means that the United States could do a lot better in this particular international competition.

Multi-party countries tend to have more women in politics, and countries with long-standing traditions of women in politics (such as the Nordic countries) also have more women in elected office. Finnish political scientist Johanna Kantola, an expert on women and politics in Europe, notes that the very first parliament for which women were allowed to run (in 1907 Finland—then a grand duchy of Russia) elected nineteen women out of a total of 200 representatives. That Finland a hundred years later has a female president and a parliament that is 42 percent female is therefore not that surprising. Change tends to happen slowly and cumulatively over time— often with two steps forwards and one step back—but imagine what might have happened if some enterprising Finnish journalist in 1907 had written about those nineteen women as a sign of women's lesser political ambition.

The United States doesn't have as long a history of women's participation in electoral politics. Ninety of the 246 women who have ever served in the U.S. Congress are current members; there are still Americans alive who were born before women had the right to vote. In short, the story of women's participation in the U.S. political scene is at its early stages, and it is far too premature to account for the dearth of women by using biological excuses.

Losing Women's Life Experiences

But would such excuses have any place even if they were true? Suppose that women indeed were less eager to wage political warfare, less eager to fight negative campaigns, less thick-skinned altogether. Would that justify a collective shrugging of shoulders about the numbers of women in elected office? Or might we ask ourselves whether a representative democratic system can truly represent all of its citizens if the game itself is rigged in a way that only appeals to some of us? Is it really necessary to see politics as "war by other means" or to arrange politics in such a way that someone with childcare obligations cannot fully participate—at least not without getting attacked for that very participation?

What is it that we might be losing if we decided on that course? Media critic Caryl Rivers says we might lose the life experience women have of the issues that tend to matter more for women than for men. "Because of the ways gender still affects our roles in life, women are more likely to pay attention to issues such as childcare and eldercare." We would lose certain points of view on matters that are brought up in the political process, and we might miss some important issues altogether. This will remain true as long as certain aspects of our life experiences are gendered, whether the reasons for such gendering are cultural or biological or both.

Anyone who followed the [US Supreme Court Justice] Clarence Thomas hearings in the early 1990s remembers that men and women had, on average, very different experiences and attitudes concerning the phenomenon of sexual harassment, and so one may also realize that a mostly-male Congress might not be the best body to create laws which reflect diverse perspectives.

Citizens of other countries have learned that much through experience. Kantola argues that in Finland, women's early participation in electoral politics influenced the introduction of a national pensions system and the public support of childcare in ways which might not have happened without the direct input from elected female representatives.

Women may also be treated more nastily than men in those campaigns, if not by the competition, then by the press.

Still not convinced of the importance of having more women run for office in the United States? Then imagine this: Suppose that only 16 percent of U.S. Congresspeople were male, that only 18 percent of state governors were men, that men were a mere 24 percent of state legislators and only 10 percent of big-city mayors. Given that nearly 50 percent of all Americans are men, doesn't that sound pretty unrepresentative to you? Yet when the same numbers are applied to women (who are more than 50 percent of all Americans), we are willing to entertain the idea that women just lack "political ambition."

The Hillary Clinton Treatment

And what happens when women do have political ambition? They get the Hillary Clinton treatment. The calls for her to quit the [2008] Democratic Primary started early and grew louder over time. Andrew O'Hagan wrote in early April: "The people seem to know well enough, and the time has come for Hillary Clinton to show that her beliefs are stronger than her ambitions, by making way for the Democrat who can win the presidency." Anne Applebaum chimed in with this in May: "If you've found the election hard to follow of late, that's because the only real issue at stake is Hillary Clinton's extraordinary, irrational, overwhelming ambition."

Perhaps her ambition was labeled as "extraordinary and irrational" at least partly because women are not supposed to have it. "Nice" women are *supposed* to bow out when asked nicely. Isn't that the reason why it was so very easy for Ruth Marcus to misread the Brookings study as saying something about women's innate ambition rather than about the process by which people decide to run—a process which presents different obstacles to men and women? Isn't that perhaps one reason why Hillary Clinton's determination to stay in the race caused so much rage on many blogs and in many columns? Political ambition is neither "nice" nor "ladylike."

Glass ceilings are better understood as internalized knowledge about the very real cultural and gender-based obstacles women in American politics have to face.

We can't answer these questions on the basis of Clinton's media treatment alone. She is, after all, only one woman. Maybe other women will not be treated so harshly when they compete strongly in an equally important race. Certainly we'll get the answers in time, assuming that more and more women run for the highest electoral office. The catch-22, though, is that women across the country have seen how the media treated Clinton, and for women considering careers in politics, the threat of being treated similarly may be a significant deterrent. The Lawless and Fox study found that women are more likely than men to worry about the nasty aspects of political campaigns. What the study did not point out is that women may also be treated more nastily than men in those campaigns, if not by the competition, then by the press.

Removing the Obstacles

It could be that all women carry little glass ceilings inside their heads, which stop them reaching for the stars. It could be. But those glass ceilings are better understood as internalized knowledge about the very real cultural and gender-based obstacles women in American politics have to face. There are equality-minded women and men trying to remove some of the institutional blockades, and we can support those efforts through advocacy organizations such as the *White House Project, She Should Run* and *Emily's List*. These organizations encourage women to run and provide them with crucial information and support. They fill up the "encouragement gap" detailed in the Lawless and Fox study.

We can also work to make sure that women with children are not handicapped at the starting lines of the political races. We can make sure that childcare is available for all families and that reasonable working hours are mandated. We can provide alternative voices when the media portrays female politicians as poor mothers or when the criticism of a female politician has sexist undertones. We can cast a critical eye on various political customs and institutions and ask if they affect all politicians equally or if they were something created when politics was an all-male sport, with then unforeseen negative consequences for women running today.

All this will help to punch holes in those glass ceilings, whether internalized or not.

We Must Actively Recruit More Women to Run for Political Office

Jennifer Lawless

Jennifer Lawless is an associate professor in the department of government at American University, where she also serves as director of the Women & Politics Institute. She is the author of the 2005 book, It Takes a Candidate: Why Women Don't Run for Office. *In 2006, she ran unsuccessfully for the US House of Representatives in the Rhode Island Democratic primary elections.*

Over the course of the past few years, I have surveyed and interviewed nearly 4,000 people who we might consider "eligible candidates"—highly successful individuals who occupy the professions most likely to precede a career in politics. Although about 50 percent of the people I spoke to had considered running for office, women were more than one-third less likely than men to have considered a candidacy. And they were only half as likely as men to have taken any of the actions that usually precede a campaign—like investigating how to place their name on the ballot, or discussing running with potential donors, party or community leaders, or even mentioning the idea to family members or friends. If we focus only on the 50 percent of people who *had* thought about running, women were one-third less likely than men to throw their hats into the ring and enter actual races.

We can't really begin to figure out how to minimize the gender gap in political ambition if we don't understand its roots. I'd like to share my experiences as a woman candidate in a state with a poor history of electing women and a very male-dominated political establishment. I'd like to begin a

Jennifer Lawless, "Why More Women Don't Hold Office," AFL-CIO Media Center, 2011. www.aflcio.org. Reproduced by permission.

conversation about political ambition, why men have it, and why women don't. And I'd like to hope that we can use the results of my research and my experiences to guide us in thinking about how to incorporate more women into the political sphere.

Women in Office—Then and Now

It's true that over the course of the past 20 years, the number of women in Congress has more than tripled. Since the end of World War II, the number of women serving in the U.S. House of Representatives and the Senate has grown by more than 800 percent. In fact, California's Democratic congressional delegation, which is the largest state party delegation in Congress, is comprised of more women than men. Things aren't so bad, right?

Wrong. The United States ranks 82nd worldwide in the percentage of women in our national legislature. Even after the gains women made this election cycle, 84 percent of the members of the House and Senate are male. Eighty-two percent of state governors are male. Seventy-eight percent of state legislators throughout the country are male. Eighty percent of big city mayors are male. And the last several election cycles indicate a plateau in both Democratic and Republican women's entry into the political sphere. Further, a recent national study of college students found that men are nearly twice as likely as women to say they might be interested in running for office at some point in the future. Voter bias against women candidates also appears to be on the rise: nearly one in every four Americans agree that "Most men are better suited emotionally for politics than are most women."

The prospects for women's full inclusion in our political system, in other words, are looking increasingly bleak. It makes sense, then, to turn to the women who are well situated to consider running for office, assess what's holding them back and work to alleviate these barriers. Based on my research,

I've identified three basic barriers women face; family roles, what it means to be a "qualified" candidate and recruitment efforts.

Family Roles

Prominent female politicians, like vice presidential candidate Geraldine Ferraro in 1984 and California gubernatorial candidate Dianne Feinstein in 1990, had to answer for the conduct of their children and spouses. Yet examples of male politicians having to offer a public defense and justification of their parenting skills or family life are far less common. Women who enter the public sphere, therefore, often face a "double bind" that men rarely need to reconcile. This double bind is something that's clearly familiar to women who are well-positioned to run for public office today. Of the people I interviewed, women were about twice as likely as men to be single, separated or divorced. They also were 20 percent less likely than men to have children. Hardly surprising, since being a wife or mother can impede professional achievement.

Sixty percent of men, but less than 40 percent of women, think they're qualified to run for office [even if they have] . . . the exact same credential and qualifications.

In families where both adults are working, generally in high-level careers, women are 12 times more likely than men to be responsible for the majority of household tasks, and more than 10 times more likely to be responsible for the majority of child care responsibilities. As a businesswoman from Chicago says: "Women are responsible not only for the family but also for earning half the money. Now we're also supposed to run for office? How much can you possibly ask?"

Perceptions of Qualifications

An active member of the Sacramento County Taxpayers League described a recent exchange with a woman who he thinks would make an excellent candidate. He said: "She is an all-American athlete, Phi Beta Kappa, Rhodes scholar finalist, Harvard Law grad and adviser to the president. I met with her for dinner the other night and basically begged her to run for office. She told me she doesn't think she's qualified. She'd never consider running. I don't get it. Who is qualified if she's not?"

> *Unlike men, well-positioned women potential candidates are significantly less likely than men to report being tapped to run for office.*

Sixty percent of men, but less than 40 percent of women, think they're qualified to run for office. Keep in mind that these men and women have the exact same credential and qualifications. They just don't perceive them this way. But it gets worse—not only do these women think that they're not qualified to run, but they also are more likely to let their doubts hold them back. A woman who doesn't think she is qualified to run for office has less than a 25 percent chance of even thinking about running. The average man who doesn't think he's qualified still has about a 60 percent chance of contemplating throwing his hat into the ring.

Gender bias and sexism heighten women's inclinations to doubt their abilities. After all, they are accustomed to operating in an environment where they feel they face a double standard and a doubting atmosphere. It follows that even women who think they are qualified to run for public office believe they need to be more qualified than men just to compete evenly. In fact, women who think they're qualified to run for public office tend to state very specific credentials. In contrast, most men do not make specific linkages between their professions and the political environment. Instead, they reference passion, leadership, and vision. An attorney from Oklahoma captured this distinction well when he explained that

"All you need is the desire to serve. That makes you qualified for the job. You can learn the details of policymaking later."

Recruitment

Unlike men, well-positioned women potential candidates are significantly less likely than men to report being tapped to run for office. The accomplished and politically engaged women I spoke with were about twice as likely as men to never have had a political leader suggest they explore running for office. Four successful women attorneys in their forties, for example, all state that they follow politics closely. All belong to political interest groups. And all contribute to political campaigns. Yet not one has ever received even the mildest suggestion to run for office. In fact, women I surveyed were one-third less likely than men to have been recruited—ever—to run for office from a party leader, elected official, or political activist.

Most easily, realistically, and concretely, we must recruit more women to run for office.

But now let me turn to the good news. Potential candidates who receive the suggestion to run for office are more than four times as likely as those who receive no such support to think seriously about a candidacy. And women are just as likely as men to respond positively to recruitment messages. For many, recruitment from political leaders serves as the key ingredient in fomenting their thoughts of running. An attorney from Connecticut commented that her interest in running for office stemmed directly from party leaders' interest in her as a candidate: "I considered running [for the legislature] because Democratic Party leaders suggested that I do it. You need to have the party's support in order to have a viable run for any office. It wouldn't have occurred to me without the suggestion from the party."

Comments from women and men who have been recruited reflect how party support brings the promise of an organization that will work on behalf of a candidate. Statements from those who have not received political support for a candidacy demonstrate that, without encouragement, a political candidacy feels far less feasible. External support is important to potential candidates from all political parties and professional backgrounds. But women are significantly less likely than men to receive it.

Here's How We Can Take Action

We must think creatively about how to integrate family with politics, as well as be cognizant of the double bind that even highly successful, professional women face. We must identify and condemn the kind of sexist behavior that leads women to feel that they must be twice as good to get half as far in the political sphere.

But perhaps most easily, realistically, and concretely, we must recruit more women to run for office. The AFL-CIO [American Federation of Labor and Congress of Industrial Organizations, a federation of 57 national and international unions] and its affiliates' political programs, for instance, are committed to increasing the number of public officials concerned about working families. Since 1996, the federation has actively worked to elect pro-worker candidates and actively assist union members running for public office. And union members are winning their elections. Currently, more than 3,000 union members hold elected office.

But that's not all. We need to go to high schools and colleges and encourage girls and women to engage in politics. Every time any of us runs across a woman who seems to fit the bill, we need to tell her—and we need to tell her more than once—that she should consider running for office. If she needs to hear it 17 times before it sinks in, then we need to tell her 17 times.

The stakes are too high for us to sit back and not aggressively fight to convince more women to enter electoral politics. The Senate Judiciary Committee never again will grill a woman who charges a man with sexual harassment the way they did Anita Hill [against Clarence Thomas in 1991] because one woman—Dianne Feinstein—now serves [as Senator from California] as one of the committee's 19 members and 15 other women serve with her in the Senate. Policies surrounding gender equity, day care, flex time, abortion, minimum wage increases and food stamps will continue to receive attention only if we elect more women legislators, because they are the most likely to prioritize these issues.

Deeply embedded patterns of traditional family roles, perceptions of what it means to be a qualified candidate, and a gender gap in political recruitment make politics a much less likely path for women than men. But it doesn't have to remain this way. It's up to us to change these dynamics, and that's the challenge that I issue to all of us.

A Team Approach Is Needed to Encourage More Women to Run for Office

Kevin Drum

Kevin Drum is a political blogger for Mother Jones.

A new paper ["Can Teams Help to Close the Gender Competition Gap?" by researchers Andrew Healy and Jennifer Pate] uses a clever design to figure out if women are more willing to compete in teams than as individuals. The answer, in a laboratory test setting, is a resounding yes:

- Even though men and women performed equally well on the task, 81% of men chose to compete as individuals compared with 28% of women.

- When participants competed in teams, the gender competition gap shrank by 31 percentage points to 22%, with 67% of men choosing to enter the competition compared with 45% of women.

One of the clever parts of the study design was a series of different competitions that tried to untease the cause of different gender preferences. The result, say the authors, is that it really is a true difference in competitive preference, not just an artifact of risk aversion, feedback aversion, or confidence. Does this make a difference in the real world? Sure it does:

> Countries that have party-list proportional representation, in which voters select a slate of candidates put forth by a party, generally have more than twice the female representation rate in their legislatures than countries that have single-

member districts. Two countries that elect some members under each system, Germany and New Zealand, illustrate the differences most clearly. In the 1994 German election, 13% of the representatives elected from single-member districts were women, while 39% of the representatives elected from party-list districts were women. In New Zealand in 1996, the corresponding numbers were 15% and 45% for the single-member and party-list districts, respectively. These differences occur primarily because women are more likely to be candidates under proportional representation.

As I recall, we have much the same phenomenon in the United States. Once they decide to run, women generally do as well as men in political campaigns. The problem is that not very many are willing to run.

Our political system isn't likely to improve this situation, but this research does suggest there might be slate-oriented ways to get more women to run. Here's an example from my neck of the woods. In my hometown of Irvine, [California] for historical reasons, there are basically two slates of candidates that run as a group for city council every couple of years. . . . This system, accidental though it is, seems to attract a fair number of female candidates. People actually vote for councilmembers individually, and usually we end up with some winners from one slate and some from another. Nonetheless, merely running as part of a team seems to encourage more female participation.

That's just my impression, of course, and it might be wrong. But it might be worth another study to see if slate-like behavior, whether formal or informal, increases the number of women who run for political office in the United States.

Organizations to Contact

The editors have compiled the following list of organizations concerned with the issues debated in this book. The descriptions are derived from materials provided by the organizations. All have publications or information available for interested readers. The list was compiled on the date of publication of the present volume; the information provided here may change. Be aware that many organizations take several weeks or longer to respond to inquiries, so allow as much time as possible.

Center for American Women and Politics (CAWP)
Eagleton Institute of Politics, Rutgers
The State University of New Jersey, 191 Ryders Ln.
New Brunswick, NJ   08901-8557
(732) 932-9384 • fax: (732) 932-6778
website: www.cawp.rutgers.edu

The CAWP is part of the Eagleton Institute of Politics at Rutgers, The State University of New Jersey. It conducts scholarly research and collects current data about American women's participation in politics with the goal of improving women's influence and leadership in public life. The CAWP website is a source of fact sheets, graphics, and other information organized both by topic and by level of office, as well as research that focuses on the status and impact of political women. Two recent research reports typify CAWP publications—"Life's a Party: Do Political Parties Help or Hinder Women?" and "Organizing American Politics, Organizing Gender."

International Women's Democracy Center
1726 M St. NW, Suite 1100, Washington, DC   20036
(202) 530-0563 • fax: (202) 530-0564
e-mail: info@iwdc.org
website: www.iwdc.org

Founded in 1995, the International Women's Democracy Center aims to strengthen women's global leadership through training, education, networking, and research. Its main focus is on increasing the participation of women leaders in politics, policy, and decision-making in governments around the world. The Center publishes a biannual newsletter called *Altering the Landscape*, which can be accessed on the center's website.

League of Women Voters

1730 M St. NW, Suite 1000, Washington, DC   20036-4508
(202) 429-1965 • fax: (202) 429-0854
website: www.lwv.org

The League of Women Voters is a nonpartisan, grassroots political organization that seeks to educate and register voters, improve elections, and improve governments. The League is currently focused on issues such as money in elections, the District of Columbia's lack of voting rights, voter registration and elections, climate change, and health care defense, but a search of the organization's website leads the reader to a number of resources relating to women and politics, including the video "Women as Candidates."

National Democratic Institute (NDI)

455 Massachusetts Ave. NW, 8th Floor
Washington, DC   20001-2621
(202) 728-5500 • fax: (888) 875-2887
website: www.ndi.org

The NDI is a nonprofit, nonpartisan organization that seeks to support and strengthen democratic institutions worldwide through citizen participation, transparency, and accountability in government. NDI supports the equitable participation of women in politics and government as an essential part of building and sustaining democracy. NDI publishes a *Win with Women* newsletter and its website is a source of news and information about women's struggles for democracy around the world. Recent examples include *Women in Kazakhstan Seek Equality at Executive Levels* and *Campaign Schools Prepare Egyptian Women to Run for Office.*

National Organization for Women (NOW)
1100 H St. NW, 3rd floor, Washington, DC   20005
(202) 628-8669 • fax: (202) 785-8576
website: www.now.org

NOW is the largest organization of feminist activists in the United States. Founded in 1966, NOW's goal is to bring about equality for all women in all sectors of society—the workplace, schools, and elsewhere. NOW works to eliminate discrimination and harassment against women; secure abortion, birth control, and reproductive rights for all women; end violence against women; eradicate racism, sexism, and homophobia; and promote equality and justice in our society. A search of the NOW website leads to blogs, election sites, endorsements, and other information relevant to women in politics.

National Women's Political Caucus
PO Box 50476, Washington, DC   20091
(202) 785-1100 • fax: (202) 370-6306
website: www.nwpc.org

The National Women's Political Caucus was founded in 1971 following Congress' failure to pass the Equal Rights Amendment by prominent women such as feminist Gloria Steinem, former Congresswoman Shirley Chisholm, and former Congresswoman Bella Abzug. The organization is dedicated to increasing women's participation in all areas of political and public life—as elected and appointed officials, delegates to national party conventions, judges in the state and federal courts, and as lobbyists, voters, and campaign organizers. The group's website is a rich source of news, research, links to numerous organizations and media websites, and legislative updates on issues important to women and politics. Linked articles, for example, include: "Women's Court: President Obama Knows He Can't Reshape the Supreme Court Ideologically, But He Can Change Its Gender Balance" and "Keep Abortion Safe and Legal? Yes. Make It Rare? Not the Point."

Pew Research Center

1615 L St. NW, Suite 700, Washington, DC   20036
(202) 419-4300 • fax: (202) 419-4349
website: www.pewresearch.org

The Pew Research Center is a nonpartisan organization that provides facts and data on the issues, attitudes, and trends shaping America and the world. It conducts public opinion polls and social science research, reports and analyzes news, and holds forums and briefings, but it does not take positions on policy issues. A search of the center's website produces a number of publications relevant to the issue of women in politics. Two examples are: "Men or Women: Who's the Better Leader?" and "Revisiting the Mommy Wars After Palin: Politics, Gender and Parenthood."

Running Start

2 Wisconsin Cir., Suite 700, Chevy Chase, MD   20815
(240) 235-6013 • fax: (240) 235-6012
e-mail: info@runningstartonline.org
website: www.runningstartonline.org

Running Start, founded in 2007, is an organization that grew out of the nonpartisan Women Under Forty Political Action Committee (WUFPAC), which financially supports young women running for federal office. The group's mission is to educate girls and young women about politics and encourage them to consider careers in politics and public office. The Running Start website offers information about the various education programs it sponsors in high schools and elsewhere, as well as news articles and a blog. Recent blog entries include "There's No Such Thing as Apolitical" and "Out of the Blocks: My First 10 days on Capitol Hill."

Women & Politics Institute

School of Public Affairs, The American University
4400 Massachusetts Ave. NW, Washington, DC   20016
(202) 885-1000
website: www.american.edu/spa/wpi

147

The Women & Politics Institute, part of American University's School of Public Affairs, seeks to close the gender gap in US political leadership. The institute provides academic and practical training to young women, encourages them to become involved in politics, and helps to sponsor research on the challenges that women face in the political arena. The institute publishes a newsletter and the group's website provides links to various news items, as well as blogs and other writings by Jennifer L. Lawless, the institute's director. One example is a recent book review, "Political System Still Failing Women and Women Candidates, Book Finds."

Bibliography

Books

Rogaia Mustafa Abusharaf — *Transforming Displaced Women in Sudan: Politics and the Body in a Squatter Settlement.* Chicago: University of Chicago Press, 2009.

Joanne C. Bamberger — *PunditMom's Mothers of Intention: How Women & Social Media Are Revolutionizing Politics in America.* Houston, TX: Bright Sky Press, 2011.

Jean Shinoda Bolen — *Urgent Message from Mother: Gather the Women, Save the World.* York Beach, ME: Conari Press, 2005.

Robert W. Cherny, Mary Ann Irwin, and Ann Marie Wilson, eds. — *California Women and Politics: From the Gold Rush to the Great Depression.* Lincoln: University of Nebraska Press, 2011.

Julie Anne Dolan, Melissa M. Deckman, and Michele L. Swers — *Women and Politics: Paths to Power and Political Influence,* 2nd ed. Upper Saddle River, NJ: Longman, 2010.

Lynne E. Ford — *Women and Politics: The Pursuit of Equality,* 3rd ed. Boston: Wadsworth, Cengage Learning, 2011.

Joyce Gelb and Marian Lief Palley, eds. — *Women and Politics around the World: A Comparative History and Survey.* Santa Barbara, CA: ABC-CLIO, 2009.

Kathy Groob   *Pink Politics: The Woman's Practical Guide to Winning Elections.* Covington, KY: November Strategies Publishing, 2011.

Sarah L. Henderson and Alana S. Jeydel   *Women and Politics in a Global World.* New York: Oxford University Press, 2009.

Torben Iversen and Frances Rosenbluth   *Women, Work, and Politics: The Political Economy of Gender Inequality.* New Haven, CT: Yale University Press, 2010.

Anne E. Kornblut   *Notes from the Cracked Ceiling: Hillary Clinton, Sarah Palin, and What It Will Take for a Woman to Win.* New York: Crown, 2009.

Mona Lena Krook   *Quotas for Women in Politics: Gender and Candidate Selection Reform Worldwide.* New York: Oxford University Press, 2009.

Mona Lena Krook and Sarah Childs, eds.   *Women, Gender, and Politics: A Reader.* New York: Oxford University Press, 2010.

Madeleine Kunin   *Pearls, Politics, and Power: How Women Can Win and Lead.* White River Junction, VT: Chelsea Green Publishing, 2008.

Jennifer L. Lawless and Richard L. Fox   *It Still Takes A Candidate: Why Women Don't Run for Office*, revised ed. New York: Cambridge University Press, 2010.

Nancy E. McGlen, et al.   *Women, Politics, and American Society.* Upper Saddle River, NJ: Longman, 2010.

Dee Dee Myers   *Why Women Should Rule the World.* New York: Harper-Collins, 2008.

Pamela Paxton and Melanie M. Hughes   *Women, Politics, and Power: A Global Perspective.* Los Angeles; Pine Forge Press, 2007.

Barbara Roberts   *Up the Capitol Steps: A Woman's March to the Governorship.* Corvallis: Oregon State University Press, 2011.

Rebecca Traister   *Big Girls Don't Cry: The Election That Changed Everything for American Women.* New York: Free Press, 2010.

Sanam Vakil   *Women and Politics in the Islamic Republic of Iran: Action and Reaction.* New York: Continuum, 2011.

Lois Duke Whitaker   *Women in Politics: Outsiders or Insiders?: A Collection of Readings,* 5th ed. Upper Saddle River, NJ: Longman, 2011.

Periodicals and Internet Sources

Kari Andren   "Despite Gains, Women Remain Minority in Pennsylvania Politics," *Centre Daily Times,* July 22, 2011. www.centredaily.com.

Christian Science Monitor   "Notable Women in US Politics," May 10, 2010. www.csmonitor.com.

Kira Cochraine   "Is Iceland the Best Country for Women?" *The Guardian*, October 3, 2011. www.guardian.co.uk.

Patrick Corcoran   "Mexico's Women Make Gains in Politics," *World Politics Review*, July 7, 2009. www.worldpoliticsreview.com.

Angela Cummine   "Should Feminists Back Michele Bachmann," *The Guardian*, August 25, 2011. www.guardian.co.uk.

Tony Dokoupil   "Why Female Politicians Are More Effective," *The Daily Beast*, January 22, 2011. www.thedailybeast.com.

Audrey Ference   "Why Female Politicians Have Fewer Sex Scandals," *The L Magazine*, June 14, 2011. www.thelmagazine.com.

France24   "The Women of the 2011 Nobel Peace Prize," July 10, 2011. www.france24.com.

Jenna Goudreau   "A Few Reasons Why Women Shouldn't Go into Politics," *Forbes*, July 7, 2011. www.forbes.com.

Beth Ingalls   "Bachmann, Angle, Palin: Triumvirate of Tea Party Idiocracy," *Open Salon*, June 29, 2011. http://open.salon.com.

Beth Ingalls   "Politics and Parties: Without Equality, Far from Parity," The International Institute for Democracy and Electoral Assistance, March 8, 2010. www.idea.int

Jone Johnson
Lewis

"Gender Balance Changes in the United States Congress," About.com, January 18, 2011. http://womens history.about.com.

Noreen Malone

"Three Women in Politics Won the Nobel Peace Prize," *New York Magazine: Daily Intel*, October 7, 2011. http://nymag.com.

Ruth Marcus

"Are Women in Politics Making Two Steps Forward, One Step Back?" *Washington Post*, April 5, 2011. www.washingtonpost.com.

Leslie Marshall

"Bachmann's Gaffes and Lies Mean She's Unfit for White House," *U.S. News & World Report*, June 29, 2011. www.usnews.com.

Susan Milligan

"Women in Congress Lose Ground in 2010 Elections," *U.S. News & World Report*, November 11, 2010. www.usnews.com.

Frank Newport

"Women More Likely to Be Democrats, Regardless of Age," Gallup.com, June 12, 2009. www.gallup.com.

Princeton
University

"Report of the Steering Committee on Undergraduate Women's Leadership," March 2011. www .princeton.edu.

Grace Rauh

"Female Politicians Make Big Strides but Continue to Struggle," *NY1*, March 28, 2011. www.ny1.com.

Julianne Escobedo Shepherd — "Congress Comprised of Fewest Women in 30 Years," *AlterNet*, November 5, 2010. www.alternet.org.

Peter J. Smith — "Pro-Life Women Make Big Gains in Congress, Governorships," LifeSiteNews.com, November 4, 2010. www.lifesitenews.com.

Susan Brooks Thistlethwaite — "Nobel Peace Prize 2011: Peace Is Women's Work," *Washington Post*, October 11, 2011. www.washington post.com.

Doug Weber — "Men Still Dominate Campaign Fund-raising Despite Women's Political Gains," *Open Secrets Blog*, November 3, 2009. www.opensecrets .org.

Joan Williams — "Retracting Our Claws on Palin and Bachmann," *Huffington Post*, June 19, 2011. www.huffingtonpost.com.

Index

121